Dermot Kavanagh is the Sports Picture Editor of the *Sunday Times*. His writing has been published in the *Sunday Times*, as well as the football magazines *When Saturday Comes* and *Howler*, and he is a contributor to the literary website London Fictions. He lives in London with his wife and three sons.

DIFFERENT CLASS

The Story of Laurie Cunningham

Dermot Kavanagh

Unbound

This edition first published in 2017

Unbound
6th Floor Mutual House, 70 Conduit Street, London W1S 2GF

www.unbound.com

© Dermot Kavanagh, 2017

Text Design by Ellipsis

A CIP record for this book is available from the British Library

ISBN 978-1-78352-376-4 (limited edition)
ISBN 978-1-78352-377-1 (trade hbk)
ISBN 978-1-78352-378-8 (ebook)

Printed in Great Britain by Clays Ltd, St Ives plc

For Hilary, Arthur, Frank and Jimmy
'local man finally finishes book'

'He'll be greatly missed by me and by all kinds of people because you'll never, ever get a champion like that again. He's one in ten, hundred, million, thousand, billion, trillion, you know, and that's my brother Laurence Paul Cunningham, and he'll live with me for ever ... *Jah Rastafari.*'

Keith Cunningham

Dear Reader,

The book you are holding came about in a rather different way to most others. It was funded directly by readers through a new website: Unbound. Unbound is the creation of three writers. We started the company because we believed there had to be a better deal for both writers and readers. On the Unbound website, authors share the ideas for the books they want to write directly with readers. If enough of you support the book by pledging for it in advance, we produce a beautifully bound special subscribers' edition and distribute a regular edition and e-book wherever books are sold, in shops and online.

This new way of publishing is actually a very old idea (Samuel Johnson funded his dictionary this way). We're just using the internet to build each writer a network of patrons. Here, at the back of this book, you'll find the names of all the people who made it happen.

Publishing in this way means readers are no longer just passive consumers of the books they buy, and authors are free to write the books they really want. They get a much fairer return too – half the profits their books generate, rather than a tiny percentage of the cover price.

If you're not yet a subscriber, we hope that you'll want to join our publishing revolution and have your name listed in one of our books in the future. To get you started, here is a £5 discount on your first pledge. Just visit unbound.com, make your pledge and type **Laurie5** in the promo code box when you check out.

Thank you for your support,

Dan, Justin and John
Founders, Unbound

CONTENTS

FOREWORD

THEN LAURIE CUNNINGHAM CAME ALONG

Ian Wright

Before I'd turned professional, when I was playing Sunday mornings, Laurie Cunningham was the player who stuck out for me. It was the same for all the guys I grew up playing football with. As youngsters we knew all the black players, Cyrille Regis, Garth Crooks, Viv Anderson and so on, then Clyde Best and Ade Coker from back in the day – and although we were very pleased they were there, as footballers they didn't mean that much. They were very good, but they were very straightforward – into him, lay it off, give and go ... that sort of stuff – we even used to say they played like white guys. Then Laurie Cunningham came along.

Laurie played how we saw black guys playing football, anywhere, on any level: Sunday morning, at school, in a scrimmage game, down on the rec. He had the skills, but most importantly he had that swagger, he had that 'vibe'. He played like we'd play; of course there was some showing off involved, but it was all about freedom and enjoyment and celebrating what you could do. Laurie was the first to bring that sort of strut to that level of professional football and he was like a magnet for us.

I remember back in the late seventies, I was fourteen or fifteen, and I saw the highlights of this game where West Brom absolutely annihilated Manchester United winning

5–3 at Old Trafford. Laurie tore the full back Stewart Houston to shreds in that game. Years later Stewart was my coach at Arsenal and I used to tease him about what Laurie Cunningham did to him that day! But for me that game was it; I was absolutely transfixed by everything he did. We all were.

When he went to Real Madrid he'd take corners with the outside of his foot, which is a ridiculous skill in itself, but he'd do it with the outside of his right foot, then go over to the other side and take one with the outside of his left foot. That was such a black brother thing to do – 'I can do that because I can do that!' – all of my mates started trying it. Because that was it; we looked at Laurie Cunningham and thought he was the one, the guy we all wanted to be like, a proper representation of how a London black guy is and how he should be playing football.

He was the same off the pitch as well, he was always well dressed, he could dance like anything, he had that same 'swagger'; in fact that was who he was and he brought that on to the pitch with him. This was as much a part of the impression he made as what he did as a player – there was a generation of black players coming through and Laurie showed them you could be yourself, that you could express yourself like that on and off the pitch. By the time I came in, almost ten years later, it was so much easier to be yourself and to be proud of it – guys like myself and Tony Finnigan and Andy Gray at Palace didn't care what people thought of us. Laurie Cunningham started all that off because he was like that anyway and didn't compromise any of his character in anything he did.

The first time I met him was at a testimonial when he

was playing for Wimbledon towards the end of the eighties. It was Alan Cork's testimonial and I was part of the all-star opposition. I don't usually play in testimonials, and the only reason I did that one was because Laurie was in the team. When he was on the bench I said hello to him, then afterwards I remember him looking really cool in this long black leather coat and me literally not being able to speak. I remember Tony Finnigan saying to me, 'Go on, go over and talk to him', but I was so in awe I couldn't talk, I just didn't know what to say. Now, I would hate for somebody to be like that with me, because it would have meant so much to me to have sat down with him and had a ten-minute chat about how I should attack this career I was just setting out on. It was a missed opportunity and something I regret to this day.

Laurie provided a shining light for so many of the second wave of black players coming through in the eighties, that – when you look at how it ended for him – it was such a shame he didn't get to see them blossom. I would have loved Laurie Cunningham to have seen me at my height; and for him to have seen the other guys – who had grown up watching him, and modelled their approach to the game on him – make it to the promised land, as it were. That would have been the icing on the cake, because I'm sure that if it hadn't been for him we wouldn't have been able to have played like we did as professionals.

PROLOGUE

On 20 April 1968, Enoch Powell made his infamous 'Rivers of Blood' speech about commonwealth immigration to an audience at a Conservative association in Birmingham. The timing was carefully chosen as it was delivered on the eve of the Parliamentary debate on the new Race Relations Bill. The Bill which proposed outlawing racial discrimination in housing and employment – and intended to make signs such as 'No Blacks, No Irish, No Dogs' on boarding house windows a thing of the past – appalled Powell who objected to the legal protection it afforded immigrants and their families. In his view, it favoured blacks over whites and by adding the concept of racial discrimination to the statute book, Parliament would be creating a privilege for 'dangerous and divisive elements' to infiltrate and dominate the population. The thought of aliens attaining the same legal rights as native British citizens unsettled Powell and he conjured up a vision of a racially divided nation, 'whole towns will be occupied by different sections of the immigrant and immigrant-descended population,' he predicted. To prevent this he proposed a policy of repatriation or 're-emigration' as he termed it, 'in short, suspension of immigration and encouragement of re-emigration hang together, logically and humanly,' he argued. The following day he was dismissed by his leader Edward Heath and shunned by mainstream conservatives for evermore – but in one sense Powell had succeeded. As a prominent public figure he gave currency to extreme views not heard so openly in Britain since before the War and expressed what many whites dared not say out loud. After his sacking London dockers and Smithfield porters called a one-day strike in protest and marched to Parliament under the banner 'Back Britain not Black Britain', and his plan for re-emigration gave licence to xenophobes to jeer and chant 'send 'em back' at far-right rallies for years afterwards. To many whites Powell was a prophet who went unrecognised in his own land and 'Powellism' continued to exert a strong hold on the psyche of the right wing of the Tory party for years to come. His definition of who was and was not a British citizen, and thus entitled to the protection of the law, posited a crucial question about identity in modern Britain. In November 1968 he further clarified his position and specifically singled out Caribbean immigrants when he said, 'the West Indian does not by being born in England become an Englishman.'

At the time of the speech Laurie Cunningham had just turned twelve years of age and, if it ever crossed his mind, probably felt as English as anyone else who had been born in London. He grew up in working-class north Islington – an area with a large West Indian population. His parents arrived in London from Jamaica in the 1950s and by the late 1960s had done well enough to buy their first house. Both found employment locally in jobs that were secure, during a time of near full employment, and living in an area with a growing Jamaican population – where many people were in the same boat – social problems, such as discrimination, could be dealt with and eventually overcome. For people like them, the Race Relations Act, although limited in scope, suggested the world was improving and progress was possible.

But by the mid-1970s that optimism had dissipated and been succeeded by a prolonged period of economic decline and rising unemployment. Harsh social divisions and a bleak, unyielding atmosphere of pessimism permeated many inner-city areas. In Parliament and the press, the nature and make-up of society came under scrutiny as commentators and politicians diagnosed a race problem in the country. Finsbury Park, where the Cunninghams lived, was one of the poorest places in the country and life for young blacks was not straightforward – simply walking the streets, particularly in groups, invited instant suspicion from the police. A mood of surveillance, of always being watched no matter what you did, prevailed, which white teenagers simply did not experience. As tabloid newspapers identified a new breed of delinquent to demonise – the black teenage mugger who preyed on defenceless old ladies – the Metropolitan Police stepped up the use of stop and search on the streets. In one case a social worker in Islington filed a complaint against the police for assaulting a fourteen-year-old boy in their custody and reported that during the next twenty-eight days he was stopped thirty-eight times. Arrests made purely on the suspicion of intent to commit a crime under the 'sus' law – that required no evidence, witnesses or accusers to be produced – were upheld by the local magistrates court at Highbury Corner, which gained a reputation for referring cases to trial on the flimsiest of claims.

In the drive to rebuild the nation after the war, mass immigration had been encouraged and Caribbean workers were specifically recruited by the government to fill the gaps in a depleted workforce. For their sons and daughters however, who had grown up in Britain's cities, the experience was vastly different. The jobs their parents had filled were no longer available and, unlike their parents who had been educated in Caribbean schools, these children were taught in inner-city schools that were wholly unprepared to meet their needs. In Islington, black teenage joblessness was estimated to be as high as 25 per cent according to one contemporary Trade Union report, and tension – particularly between fathers and sons – led to an acute divide. The second generation who had grown up in England spoke differently from their parents and held different attitudes to religion, work and authority, and were less prepared to take what they were given by a society that treated them as outsiders and put them at the back of the queue for decent jobs.

Many school-leavers were born in the Caribbean and had only been sent for once their parents had established themselves. Being reunited after such a break must have been difficult for both parties and, with few cultural milestones to share, an inevitable distance must have been common. In the case of the Cunningham family, the two brothers Keith and Laurie had different starts in life. Keith the eldest spent his first four years in Jamaica, apart from his mother and sibling for two years, and as he grew up identified strongly with his Jamaican heritage. His younger brother who was born and bred in London, and never visited Jamaica, was more immersed in British culture through his participation in football from an early age and his father affectionately nicknamed him his 'English boy'.

The term 'Black British' had yet to be defined. For this generation it often felt like everyone was against them and when the realisation hit that they were not considered 'English' by others, confusion turned to resentment. The film-maker Don Letts who grew up in Brixton says of this time 'to most we were black bastards ... we were like a lost tribe. It was something new in the seventies and we were struggling to work out what this was.' In the sceptical world of professional football, where black players were distrusted, Laurie Cunningham needed more than talent and determination to survive; he needed a special kind of bravery, both physical and mental, and the temperament to cope in a sport where the odds were against him from the start.

1

'NOTHING SEEMED TO FAZE HIM'

The popular myth that modern multicultural Britain was born with the arrival of the transport ship HMT *Empire Windrush* at Tilbury in Essex in June 1948 is a potent one. Memorable footage caught by dockside film cameramen – with some reporters perched on car rooftops waiting for the historic moment of landing – did not, however, record a pioneering event. Caribbean immigrants had lived in Britain for many years and served in both World Wars. In the First World War, 16,000 had volunteered to fight as part of the British West Indies Regiment – the first contingent of all black soldiers in the British Army – which was established in 1915. In the Second World War 10,000 West Indians volunteered for the services and thousands more served in the Merchant Navy or worked in the factories of the industrial north. Officially *Windrush* carried 492 passengers (plus eight stowaways), the majority of whom were ex-servicemen or semi-skilled workers able to afford the £28 10s fare. Their average age was twenty-four. Newspaper advertisements placed around the Caribbean invited them to come to Britain and work for London Transport, British Rail and the health service, amongst others – to help the mother country after six years of war. A photo caption from

Planet News, one of the main news agencies of the day, reads: 'They sailed for Britain when they could not find work in their homeland. Fifty-two of them will volunteer for the Services, over two hundred have friends who can give them prospects of employment, and most of the remainder are to seek work in Britain after interviews with the Ministry of Labour. Among the party were a number of boxers, with their manager.' The last sentence is interesting. Jamaica, with the largest population of all the colonial islands in the Caribbean, supplied the greatest number of migrants to Britain. Many West Indians from smaller islands went on to settle in inner-city areas where Jamaicans had established themselves first, not because they particularly liked them, but because their presence provided a sense of security. Jamaicans had a no-nonsense reputation within the wider community and such truculence was seen as one of their best, or worst, qualities, depending on your point of view. The most forthright had the confidence to walk into a place as if they owned it, and that was one reason why many Jamaican men found employment as doormen and bouncers at West End nightclubs in the years immediately after the War.

After the dispersal of those who had arrived on the *Windrush*, there was no immediate rush of migrants in their wake. In the five years following barely a thousand crossed the Atlantic to Britain. The bulk of Caribbean migration took place in the following decade, during the late 1950s and early 1960s. During this time a quarter of a million arrived in Britain within a period of seven years, primarily as a result of two events: one in the USA and the other in Great Britain. In 1952 the US Congress passed laws that restricted immigrant numbers. Up to that point America had operated a broadly open-door policy towards migrants from the Caribbean, and Florida with its abundant fruit farms proved a cheap and popular destination for many. In Britain, the Notting Hill race riots of 1958 started a national debate about immigration and its effects on society which prompted calls for tighter border controls. When word got back to the islands that curbs were to be introduced by the British government, this stiffened the resolve and large numbers applied before the shutters were finally brought down with the passing of the Commonwealth Immigrants Act in 1962, limiting entry into Britain.

Mavis Iona Trout and Elias Cunningham met when they were teenagers in the early 1950s. She was one of four daughters of Stanford Laurence Trout, a public works foreman from St Mary's Parish north of Kingston in Jamaica. Cunningham came from Caymanas Park, the horse-racing district of the island, and was training to be a jockey. He weighed just over seven stone when the couple first met. Together they made an attractive match: he dapper and athletic, she pretty and ebullient with a beaming smile. By the age of seventeen, Mavis was pregnant and gave birth to a son, named Keith. With poor prospects in Jamaica the couple decided to book Mavis a passage to London where she had an aunt living in Islington, north London, who could help her to find work. Leaving Keith with her sisters, and with Elias determined to make a go of it as a jockey, Mavis sailed on a ship bound for Italy in 1955, accompanied by one extra undeclared passenger – she was pregnant again with the due date in the spring of the following year. Upon reaching Italy she crossed Europe by train and arrived in Southampton knowing little of what to expect of life in England.

The baby arrived on 8 March 1956 at Whittington Hospital in Archway, and was named Laurence Paul Cunningham. Mavis was living in a shared house at 3 Brookside Place, an unprepossessing cut-through that joins Holloway Road and Junction Road – just a stone's throw from the stark Victorian hospital buildings. The Jamaican community had not yet established itself to any great degree in this part of London but with female relatives nearby – in both Holloway and on Caledonian Road – Mavis could count on support. After the winners had dried up at Caymanas Park, Elias brought Keith over with him in 1958 and the family were fully reunited when the couple finally married. By the next decade the surrounding areas to the north, especially Finsbury Park and Tottenham, had become the heart of the black community in north London (there were also sizable Irish and Greek communities), and in all the years that the Cunningham family lived in London, including several changes of address, they never moved far – choosing to remain in the close-knit, working-class north London streets. For whatever reason Laurence's birth was not registered until February 1961, nearly five years after the event, perhaps because the infant Cunningham was due to start primary school and it simply had not been attended to earlier by his parents. The birth certificate is signed by Elias in a spidery, loping hand with the home address given as 30 Queen's Drive, Finsbury Park, indicating the family had moved on from the shared accommodation in Archway. Both parents were employed in manual labour. Elias's occupation is given as paint sprayer and engraver and he worked for a company based in Amwell Street, Islington. Mavis first found work at the Bristol Laundry on Holloway Road then moved on to a job at the Eagle Pencil factory in Tottenham – at the time the largest of its kind in Europe – as a packer on the production line.

By 1962 the Cunninghams had bought their first house at 6 Trinder Road off Crouch Hill in Hornsey. Leaving the pencil factory, Mavis found work at a local garment manufacturer, Classic Fabrication, where she stayed for ten years, eventually becoming a supervisor. Unusually for a black woman she owned and drove a car, indicating an aspirational and independent side to her personality. Of the two parents Elias appears the more introverted and reserved. Eustus Isiae, a school friend of eldest son Keith, who was also born in in 1954, recalls visiting the home regularly and describes the atmosphere there: 'He was just a quiet man, you'd go round the house and he was sitting there listening to his music, the old woman might be watching telly in another room, he was just a hard-working man, so most of his life was based around going to work.' The domestic setting was typically Jamaican, with a front room that was hardly used from day to day but kept instead for 'best', and was out of bounds for children. Isiae continues: 'Although it was called a living room we hardly ever went in there. We would go straight through the house and we would go to the bit next to the kitchen. The living room was a special room; at Christmas time you can go in there but most of the time you are not allowed – in there it's always immaculate.' The décor was typically Jamaican too with walls covered in a variety of contrasting wallpaper, patterned carpet, and numerous family photographs. A large reproduction painting of gondolas in Venice bought by Elias took pride of place in the living room, above vases of flowers and a collection of ornaments and decorative plates that were supplemented in later years with Laurie's trophies and medals.

Cunningham had a similar character to his father. Softly spoken and introverted as a young boy, he was a natural when it came to any sporting activity. At Pooles Park Primary School he excelled at running – both sprinting and longer distance – and was singled out as an exceptional hurdler by his games teacher. His natural fitness and native ability gave him a self-belief that he wore lightly. Mavis recalls his easy-going way and lack of arrogance when it came to his athletic talent, which he never exploited in the playground: 'He wasn't the kind of person that really go around showing up these things,' she reflects. A sensitive and imaginative boy, he possessed artistic skill which he expressed in differing ways. Mavis recalls with pride a painting he brought home one day from primary school: 'Drawing was something that he loved. I remember he'd drawn an old man and his teacher asked him, "Who is it?" and he said, "I don't know, I just draw this old man." It was really good, I've still got it hung up in my house.' Years later in a cover article for the *Sunday Times Magazine* in 1976, the doyen of football writers, Brian Glanville – a man not easily impressed – commented on the picture on display in the family home, 'On the Cunninghams' wall there hangs a strikingly well-observed portrait of an old man, painted by Laurie.'

He liked music too and had an affinity with the piano, which he taught himself to play at an early age. As in most

Jamaican households music was an integral part of daily life and an essential element at social gatherings such as wedding parties, christenings and birthdays. And where there was music, there was dancing. Given his propensities it is not hard to imagine the young Cunningham, with his casual grace, thriving in such a creative domestic environment. Mavis recalls: 'He loved dancing, he loved music. I bought him two pianos you know. I bought him one that was electrical when he was younger, then when he was older, I bought him a very big one, a stand-up one.' Returning to the theme of his love of all things sporty she adds, 'He was really good at swimming. I didn't really know he was so good at football until his teacher wrote to me and asked me to come and see. He kept telling me how good he was at football and swimming, if it wasn't football, I think it would be swimming.' It is interesting to note this relaxed versatility was apparent at such an early age, and it continued to be a character trait throughout his later life. Even as a young boy he found great pleasure in a variety of pursuits, all of which he mastered quite naturally without the need for much instruction from the adults around him.

The Cunningham brothers although close throughout their lives went in different directions early on. Keith the eldest by two years naturally looked out for his younger brother but the boys had very different temperaments. They attended Sunday school at St Mary's Church on Hornsey Rise together, and joined the Boys' Brigade where they took part in gymnastics and played in the marching band. Keith was quick to anger with a rebellious streak that got him expelled from primary school and led him into trouble with the police as a teenager that culminated in a prison sentence – but he says his brother never judged him even when he become famous. He recalls: 'He never ever said one bad word about me. We never had a rivalry, we rarely argued, it wasn't like that. As little boys we used to share the bed and he'd wet it and I woke up soaking wet, so I used to get annoyed by that. He never hung his clothes up properly. I was tidy, he was messy ... He matured mentally, football just came to him out of the blue really, he just melted into it all of a sudden. We both went to training but I didn't stick to it, I was doing my own thing by then. He loved what he was doing but he didn't big it up.'

Living in an area that was often harsh for black teenagers, Keith sums up the filial differences between the two boys when he states, 'He studied and played his football ... I went a different way.' He recalls one formative experience when the family were living in Trinder Road. The brothers were playing in the playground of a white council estate that was considered a no-go area for black children, and as soon as they were spotted by a group of local boys they were chased back home through the streets. Arriving breathless and agitated at the front door their father asked what was up and when Keith explained he insisted that Keith go back outside and fight the ringleader.

Finsbury Park had few recreational spaces compared to other, leafier London boroughs. The best places for informal football kick-abouts were Finsbury Park itself or Highgate Wood. The effects of bomb damage from the war were still visible on the streets and large craters dotted the area which offered an irresistible and impromptu playground for the curious and adventurous.

In September 1967, Cunningham left primary school and started at Highgate Wood Secondary School in Hornsey. On his first day, uncharacteristically, he got into an argument with a boy called Robert Johnson. Johnson a big, physically strong boy, who had spent his first eight years in Jamaica, commanded respect by his appearance alone. A grandfather now and speaking in his comfortable, suburban, front room in Woodford Green in north-east London, he cuts a genial figure with a smiling voice that is never too far away from a spontaneous and infectious laugh. He recalls with a still discernible Jamaican lilt: 'Laurie never fight, but he fought me on our first day. It was all about defending somebody else that I tripped over and he thought that I was wrong. I shouldn't really have done it because I was bigger. But we were best friends after five minutes.'

Johnson became the first of a series of friends in Cunningham's life who looked out for him on the football pitch. Where Cunningham was quick, balanced and skilful, Johnson was strong, fearless and resolute. Both were natural sportsmen and seemed to spark off each other with an instinctive understanding of each other's ability.

'For the first year at school I didn't play football because my mum didn't like me playing it, so for the first year I played rugby and that's where me and Laurence got together. We were very quick, we were very tricky. Nobody could catch us. Then we started to play other sports as well, cricket, basketball, we were all-rounders basically. Laurie was a better all-rounder than I was, but still we had a great friendship and we played well together in everything. He'd look for me, I'd look for him. Playing football we didn't need to look to see where each other was, we just hit the ball and knew we were going to be there. I could hit long balls to him and he could hit long balls back to me. I just knew where he was going next, it was like ball over the top, Laurie's on to it, goal.'

Apart from his talent as a sportsman Cunningham stood out in other ways too. Despite the fact he had to wear school uniform he managed to style it to his own taste. For example, the school jumper was navy blue, a colour he disliked and refused to wear throughout his life. Instead he chose to wear a black jumper which matched the black uniform trousers and highly polished shoes he favoured. If the desired effect was to get himself noticed it worked. Teenagers tend to pick up on the smallest stylistic transgression and the merest detail can have quite an impact. Johnson expands:

'Laurie always had this fashion thing even at school because he used to tie his tie differently. He was one of the first that came in with a short tie, that was his unique style, all of us used to try and blend in and tie it properly ... Laurie just had a way about him when he dressed, even with the school uniform he made it look good. Although he was in uniform he was just different. On the first day going back to school, you all want to make an impression, you'd dress up the morning you were going back into school, but when you got in the playground you'd look at one person and go "Oh God! Look at Laurie." His shoes weren't school shoes, they were patent or brogues. Anything in fashion, you name it, Laurence would have it before anyone, everybody, regardless. He always looked smart, but I had a feeling sometimes going to school that his mum did all that for him. He looked good but it wasn't him that did it, his mum sent him out like that.'

At the same time as Cunningham and Johnson started secondary school a remarkable football team was being assembled in Highgate by a forward-thinking social worker originally from Yorkshire called Bob Cottingham. Born in 1922, Cottingham had started coaching football in his mid-forties as a trainee social worker in Bermondsey, south London, where he formed a five-a-side football team for the youngsters in his care. After completing his training he began working for Islington council where he stayed for many years. The success of the Bermondsey side encouraged him to establish a similar five-a-side team closer to home in Highgate. Highgate North Hill, named after the address of the local primary school that his son attended, were formed in October 1967 and quickly transformed into an eleven-a-side team as word spread around the area.

The previous summer in 1966 England won the World Cup by beating West Germany 4–2 in a thrilling and unforgettable game at Wembley. A week after that famous victory Cottingham attended a residential Football Association coaching course at Loughborough College devised by the former England manager Walter Winterbottom. The need for a codified national coaching scheme had become paramount after the humiliating defeat suffered by England at the hands of Hungary in 1953. England were beaten, 6–3, for only the second time ever at Wembley. It was not so much the margin of the defeat as the manner of it that shocked supporters. England were inferior in every aspect. Led by the visionary Ferenc Puskás, the Hungarian side obliterated England with a dazzling display of flair and organisation that seemed to be light years ahead of the English game. In the return fixture a year later in Budapest an almost identical England team, having apparently learnt nothing, received a 7–1 drubbing. As a serious and enlightened football man, Cottingham wanted to emulate the skill and simplicity that the Hungarians had shown. His son Steve Cottingham says of his father, 'The teams that influenced him the most were the Hungarians in the 1950s, they really broke the mould, Real Madrid and to some extent the Brazilians – this was before the 1970 World Cup – who were arguably the best side ever ... my father's philosophy was you put the team out and let them play, you wouldn't tie them down with tactics or tie them down with having to treat the ball like a hot potato, and that worked.'

Real Madrid sealed their reputation as the undisputed kings of European football after a superlative performance in the 1960 European Cup Final when they beat Eintracht Frankfurt 7–1 at Hampden Park in Glasgow – their fifth consecutive victory in the competition. Fluid and devastatingly effective they epitomised the new style of European football which made the English game look geriatric by comparison. England's World Cup victory was a vindication of coaching and tactics after the Hungarian humiliation – but seemed to do as much harm as good in the years that followed. Instead of embracing individuality and flair, organisation and a desire not to concede goals became the paramount concern. Adventure was frowned upon as players were urged to stick to the game plan devised by their coaches rather than relying on their instincts as footballers. Anybody who contravened this orthodoxy was deemed to be 'unprofessional' in an age when being called a 'good professional' was the ultimate praise. A dark ages for creativity at international level followed as flair and guile perished in the face of conformity and grit.

Steve Cottingham is a friendly and engaging man who was born in 1957. Now a lawyer he remembers the first time he heard the name Laurie Cunningham. A friend came round to his house to tell him about a boy he had met at school who was interested in joining Highgate North Hill. He was an amazing winger, he said, and lived nearby in Finsbury Park. His friend was worried because he was a winger too but he brought him along to the next training session anyway. 'Laurie was just out of this world, he was dribbling around three or four of us as if it was the most natural thing in the world.' The new team was a true representation of the area and reflected Bob Cottingham's inclusive social worker beliefs. Steve adds 'we were drawn from the local community, a mixture of different backgrounds and race and class. We thought it was natural; I think it bothered other people more than it bothered us. Often a lot of sides we played were white, which coming from north London in those days was a bit odd because north London was a very mixed community, we had people from West Indian backgrounds and Greek Cypriot backgrounds all of whom reflected the community we lived in.'

Bob Cottingham said of his team 'we were just a street side, we didn't have any premises but we won the under-16 Middlesex Cup against bigger, better equipped teams' and said of the young Cunningham, 'he played the game pretty cheerfully, he never blew up ... he was a very happy and well-disposed youngster. In the team they knew who the star was, he had this remarkable skill, but he never put on side, he never carried on as though he thought he was God's gift to football; he was a well-balanced boy I always thought. I felt he could go very far in the game, he had all the talent. He had such devastating effects on the opposition that you just let him loose and you got your results.'

From the outset the club was a family affair. The Cottinghams lived in a large house on Dukes Avenue in Muswell Hill with a spacious garden that was open to all visitors. After training each Saturday the boys would go back there for orange squash and hotdogs provided by Mrs Cottingham, who also washed and ironed the kit. Boys stayed until evening playing football in the garden and often shared dinner with the family. Robert Johnson, who joined the team at the same time as Cunningham, refers to the Cottingham house as a 'home from home', but didn't mention his visits there to his mother because she disapproved so strongly of his playing football. The informal and idyllic-sounding atmosphere found there would appeal to any boy and Cunningham became a regular visitor to the Muswell Hill house. Steve Cottingham fondly recalls: 'He'd just turn up sometimes and come in and we'd get on with whatever we were getting on with. If we were going down to my grandparents in Highgate he'd join us. He just fitted in. He didn't try and adapt himself for other people, he just was who he was, he had that confidence in himself; he could find himself in any number of situations and be able to deal with it. For example, my grandparents were fairly well-off middle-class Jewish people living in Highgate and they got on really well with him. Nothing seemed to faze him. He remained the same person whatever he was doing and whoever he was with. At school I do not recall him getting into fights or trouble. Looking back he seemed to have an inner confidence which never came across as arrogance. People may have envied his astonishing ability, but no one I knew resented him. Far from it, we all wanted him to do well.'

By 1968 the Cunningham family had moved again to a three-storey house at 73 Lancaster Road near the busy Stroud Green Road in Finsbury Park. At the time the area was one of the poorest in London with an abundance of run-down, semi-derelict properties that were used as squats and houses could be bought for a couple of thousand pounds. Predominantly a West Indian and Irish neighbourhood with a tough reputation, the two communities generally got on well together – many Jamaicans shared the same Catholic faith as the Irish – but tended to keep themselves apart socially. The local pub, the Stapleton Arms – an ornate Victorian gin palace – had two main bars, one frequented by the Irish and the other by West Indians. The separation although conscious was not due to any particular ill-feeling between the two groups but more a case of how things were in a crowded working-class neighbourhood.

Highgate North Hill played in the Sunday morning Regent's Park League and Cottingham collected the boys in his Volkswagen camper van, handing out glucose tablets during the journey. He usually carried a spare pair of boots in Cunningham's size just in case, as he was prone to forget his own and usually picked him up outside the Lancaster Road house where he would be waiting, kicking a ball against a wall.

For Robert Johnson things were not so simple: 'Mr Cottingham did a lot for Laurie and a lot for me. My mum was so strict she wouldn't let me come to the football but Mr Cottingham would bring the boys down to the front gate and beg for her to let me out, and she would say "there's no future in football, there's no money in it. I want him to have a skill." But then the boys would start: "please, please!" and eventually she would let me go.'

He further praises Cottingham for his understanding of the game and the way he could read the opposition, 'Sometimes we would lose 2–0, or 2–1, but by changing it round we could beat that team. Sometimes if we were playing a very strong team he'd say to me, "Robert I know you want to play up front, but you are playing centre back, you are playing the sweeper role." He reminds me of Alex Ferguson, creative, thinking about the game all the time.'

Football now dominated both boys' lives and even if there was something else arranged for the weekend, or a family commitment, both knew that they would play it at some point during the day. In summer, marathon forty-a-side matches open to all-comers took place in Finsbury Park when boys just turned up and joined in. Games that began in the early afternoon would not end until dusk. Johnson believes that this intuitive football-for-football's sake was crucial to the development of Cunningham's touch as a player. He says, 'It was just one big game really, that's how we kept fit, you just played football continuously, seven days a week, we just loved playing football. That's when you see Laurence at his best, we'd just control the ball, pass it, you didn't see people tearing around ... at school they banned big footballs because we used to break too many windows, so we used to play with tennis balls. We would play tennis over the net, Laurie was great at that. Then the school started playing tennis football as training for the footballers, so that was great.'

Cunningham later remarked on these early days, 'I was always around black guys. We knocked the ball around in the streets. English kids seemed to rush around a shade too fast.'

In summer 1968 Cottingham organised an exotic football trip for his young team that would have a lasting effect on everybody who took part. The Highgate boys were a mixture in terms of race and social backgrounds, a few came from harsh environments, but most were drawn from ordinary families whose children went to the local comprehensive schools. Before the Channel Tunnel, continental Europe was another world and visiting it a considerable undertaking and beyond the budget of most working-class families. A day trip to France was the most many London schoolchildren experienced and to venture further afield was rare.

Cottingham organised a two-week tour to Vienna where Highgate were to play the youth teams of the city's top three sides – Rapid Vienna, Austria Vienna and Fortuna 05. Twenty boys were taken and the whole Cottingham family went along as well as it doubled up as the family summer holiday. Vienna may seem an unlikely choice but the connection was the result of a friendship made by Steve Cottingham at Highgate Primary School. He had befriended an Austrian boy called Andreas Rauscher who was a keen footballer and whose father was a diplomat. When he moved his family back to Austria in 1968 Rauscher senior, now a youth coach at Fortuna 05 in his spare time, invited Cottingham to bring his team over for a mini-tournament and combine it with a summer holiday. One of the players on the tour, Toby

Apperley, a minicab driver and photographer who now lives in South Wales – and who was by his own admission a 'live wire' as a twelve-year-old – has fond memories of the visit; and of Cottingham too, who helped his mother out when she was struggling to bring up four boys on her own. He let Apperley bring his brothers along to training at Regent's Park to give her a few precious hours break each week. Recalling the journey and arrival in Vienna, Apperley says: 'I remember after a gruelling journey by train and ferry and train again standing outside the Fortuna changing rooms at their mini stadium in the very hot sun. All the Highgate boys were lined up on one side with their luggage and the Austrian boys' parents were kind of taking their pick. Emotions were mixed, the majority of the boys had never been away from their parents for long, let alone been abroad. Now they were standing in a foreign country and being picked off by foster parents, albeit temporary ones. It was like a World War Two evacuee experience and must have been disturbing to some. There were a few incidents of nervousness and homesickness understandably, but most of us were looking at the mini stadium pitch. Although it was red gravel we didn't care, it was surrounded by high fencing with an entrance gate and cordoned off by advertising boards, for us very professional. A far cry from the multi-pitched Regent's Park with its central mass changing room.'

Split up amongst various families, the boys gathered at the house where Apperley was billeted next to the Fortuna ground for kick-abouts and visits to the adjacent park. Robert Johnson, a fussy eater, recounts cooking for the family he was with, who grew to love his speciality – Jamaican fried fish. He still clearly recalls the quality of pitches the games were played on, in marked contrast to the municipal mud heaps they were all used to in England, 'The pitches were like carpet, we just kept touching it, when you hit a pass it just kept going straight. Oh man! It was beautiful.' In the first game Highgate beat Fortuna comfortably and in the second match faced Rapid Vienna's youth team at the impressive Prater Stadium. Press interest had grown around this multi-racial outfit from London and Cunningham was singled out as the star as he was scoring most of the goals. A picture of him training appeared on the front page of a daily newspaper and tickets were even sold for the game. Television news, intrigued, interviewed him and Apperley recalls his surprise when he was referred to as 'the negro Bobby Charlton', although he appreciates it was meant as a compliment, however clumsily phrased. The Rapid Vienna match was the first time Cunningham and his teammates had played before a paying audience and both Apperley and Steve Cottingham recall a few hundred curious spectators turning up to watch. Cunningham again played a starring role in the scorching, summer heat as the game finished in an honourable 2–2 draw. Between games the boys were treated to some excursions by their hosts including a coach trip to the Alps and the local Schneeberg mountain – 'the biggest mountain seen by any of us until then was probably Muswell Hill,' Apperley quips – and a visit to the famous Prater Fair which included a ride on the Wiener Riesenrad, the biggest Ferris wheel in Europe at the time at over 200 feet high.

The Highgate boys made an impact wherever they went standing out in the neat and tidy surroundings of late 1960s

Vienna. Apperley puts it succinctly: 'Everywhere we went, whether it was an organised trip or just on our own with the Fortuna boys, people would often stop and look, it was hardly surprising really looking back. Austria was quite conservative while Britain was culturally exploding in comparison. We could be messing about in the lovely Hugo Wolf Park just behind Fortuna's ground and there would be a skinhead boy with boots and braces, a scruffy long-haired boy and Laurie flashily dressed, but more startling to onlookers, black. I didn't notice any other black people the whole time we were there.'

The tour culminated in a mini-tournament between all four teams which was won by Highgate. An official reception was held at the palatial, plushly carpeted Town Hall to mark the occasion, complete with speeches and presentations made by the Lady Mayoress. Caviar on toast was served, which some of the boys to their cost mistook for blackcurrant jam. Sadly after two weeks and laden with chocolate and gifts, the boys bid an emotional farewell to their hosts and began the long journey home. Cunningham was given a gold necklace with a small football pendant as a keepsake which he proudly showed off to his teammates. As well as chocolate the boys also brought back some new skills from their Austrian friends – Johnson recalls seeing players chest the ball down from throw-ins and flick it with the outside of their foot in one move and most memorably of all he saw the 'rainbow flick' performed for the first time. This is a complex move whereby a player beats an opponent by rolling the ball up the back of their calf muscle with the instep of their opposing foot whilst running at pace and launching it over their head and that of their opponent and leaving them for dead. Cunningham mastered it quickly as it played to his strengths: speed, balance and quick feet. Johnson states: 'We came back that summer and we tore up the league with it.' As a unit Highgate now had invaluable European experience and a strength and unity that few rivals could match.

By this time Cunningham was playing for London Schools, the district and Highgate North Hill, and professional scouts soon picked up on his eye-catching displays. Soon after the Austrian trip he was invited to train with Arsenal, his local team, two nights a week. Johnson was also part of the professional youth circuit in London and immediately both he and Cunningham came up against a different methodology to the loose, freewheeling style they had grown accustomed to under Cottingham. He says, 'We found at the professional clubs it was "give and go, give and go", but it was not always about "give and go". I would receive a ball, Laurence would receive a ball, we'd hold it and then we'd look, and beat two, three players, then give it and go, one, two go. And that's what Mr Cottingham's team was about. A lot of the players in Mr Cottingham's team were from Arsenal ... we'd play stronger teams and beat them: "Watch those two players." "That one." "Which one's Laurie Cunningham?" "I don't know." "Watch him, don't let him go down the wing." They'd kick Laurence to pieces but all Laurie had to do was "Rob, I'll find you a ball mate, just get on the end of it." And I used to get on the end of it. In Regent's Park we scored the most goals in one season, I think it was over a hundred, nobody came near to it.'

Bob Cottingham kept a record of results and press cuttings for his team and in what is probably the first mention of the name Laurie Cunningham in print, he filed away one clipping from the *Hornsey Journal* dated 2 February 1968. Headlined 'Cunningham Makes Life Easy for North Hill', it read: 'Two goals and a non-stop display by Laurie Cunningham helped Highgate North Hill boys under-12 team to a 7–1 victory over Mildmay at Regent's Park ... Cunningham collected the ball on the halfway line, swerved past three defenders and hammered an unstoppable shot from twenty-five yards ... Cunningham's speed and control should have led to more goals if the forwards had taken the chances that he created.' In another match Highgate beat hapless Gainsford 26–0.

With players on the books of professional clubs across London, Highgate hit a purple patch and won the Regent's Park League, the Haringey Cup and the F.A. Youth Cup within a couple of years. In the final of the Middlesex Cup at Sutton United's ground – played excitingly for the first time under floodlights – Cunningham was the star once again. On a full-size heavy pitch, the hard fought final ended 1–1 after ninety energy-sapping minutes. In extra time Highgate emerged victorious as 2–1 winners but the exertions had taken their toll on everyone apart from Cunningham, his strength and athleticism astonished his teammates. After such a shattering encounter, Apperley recalls: 'In the changing room after, the celebrations were subdued. All the players, although really happy, were exhausted. Most were sitting down when Laurie bounced in, he had probably been running around the pitch. He rolled his socks into a ball, counted off ten keepy-uppies and shot them against the wall. Laurie had covered more ground than any other player and would have been man of the match. It's ludicrous to think that this boy, jumping with delight after such a tough 120 minutes would, in a few years, be released by Arsenal football club citing lack of stamina.'

With five black players Highgate stood out from most of their opponents. Another black player in the team was Michael La Rose, now a lecturer on black history and culture and the son of John La Rose, the Trinidadian writer and activist who founded the New Beacon bookshop on Stroud Green Road in 1966 – a unique establishment that can claim to be London's longest running independent black bookshop.

La Rose speaks about the violence meted out to young black players at games during this time, especially in east London, an area where he says there were always problems. Fist fights on the pitch were common and black players were usually singled out for special treatment. Accordingly La Rose says you measured your teammates on how they defended you in such situations. In Cunningham's case if his speed and agility couldn't protect him then his friend Robert Johnson was more than willing to help out. It is impossible to think of teenage boys today being subjected to the kind of physical and verbal abuse that Cunningham, Johnson and La Rose were routinely exposed to – not just from their peers, but more disgracefully from snarling adults. Johnson tells of the ugly atmosphere on the touchlines at matches: 'We went through a lot of stuff. We played the semi-final of the F.A. Youth Cup in Yorkshire and we had dog shit thrown at us, bananas you know, and one guy was telling his son to break Laurie's leg and break my leg. I said, "You better shut your mouth, before your son comes off with a broken leg." Every time the dad said something I clapped that boy cos he was playing on the wing and I was right back. I hit him so hard in the end he just came

29

off. He asked his manager to take him off; he couldn't take no more and then his dad started to abuse him saying he's weak, and he was an up-and-coming England player! Me and Laurie at the end of the game were sat there laughing, cos it's an everyday thing for us you know. They thought the bananas and all of that was going to upset us, but actually we tore the hide off them ... Our parents didn't come to football but a lot of the white parents did and they used to intimidate us: "Oh, I got a baseball bat in the car for you, you don't know what I'll do after the game if you tackle my son." You know, I don't give a damn, one-time I did a Cantona and left the pitch. I knew I was going to tackle this boy but I wanted to miss him, I just wanted to hit his dad. Literally I just flew past this guy, straight into the dad, forearmed him, shut his mouth up. After that it was a wonderful game! Laurie wouldn't have done that. After he said, "Rob, that's the best thing I've ever seen you do."

The racism was not limited to the sidelines of youth football. At professional clubs there were numerous black players on schoolboy contracts who never seemed to make any progress. Flair and individualism were generally frowned upon by English coaches and a common myth grew around black players that they lacked courage and stamina, were not prepared to graft, and were somehow unprofessional. This view conveniently overlooked the fact that the two best players in the world at the time, Pelé and Eusébio (both of whom had appeared, and been much admired in England, in the 1966 World Cup finals) were black. La Rose explains his feelings of frustration at witnessing teams with talented black players, such as Highgate, winning cups in London and nationally, but never breaking through to senior level.

'There was loads of black players signed to clubs but they couldn't get past schoolboy; most of the players that came out of Highgate North Hill didn't get past schoolboy, and even he [Cunningham] didn't get past it at Arsenal, he had to sign for Leyton Orient. Other people were signed at Tottenham, Chelsea, West Ham but couldn't get past the schoolboy apprenticeship situation and you knew if you were sixteen or seventeen and you hadn't been chosen that was it.'

With most clubs operating a closed shop, La Rose was prompted to form an all-black team called The Uniques as a direct response to the situation. He realised the only way to improve things was to take matters into his own hands and do it himself. He says, 'It was kind of moving up, well, we can't get in, then let's break the door down. A lot of black players played for the Cypriot and Turkish teams too, because they got paid; they had a lot of betting on the games and through that some black players went to Cyprus, Greece and Turkey and signed for professional teams. The other route was to go to the US and get into college football. They were the options in front of you.' Cunningham occasionally earned money playing in the Turkish and Greek leagues around north London as a 'boots for hire'. Skilful players offered their services around the municipal pitches at Market Road in Islington, where a fiver or the promise of a new pair of boots could buy you a guaranteed goalscorer for the day. With big sums of money changing hands in bets, demand was always high for a tried and tested match-winner like Cunningham.

Johnson – who played in Greece for six months after offers from Tottenham, Arsenal and Chelsea failed to materialise – highlights the divide that existed between the black and the white players at professional clubs. It was not just a racial but a philosophical divide, too, one that questioned your whole approach to the game. He describes what it was like to be a black fifteen-year-old apprentice: 'We all did a youth circuit, Arsenal, Chelsea, Tottenham and so on. At Arsenal I didn't like how they treated us. You had the white and the black separate. At Tottenham we got five shillings or ten bob to go to the fish and chip shop and catch a bus home. The white guys were getting twenty-five pounds, they could take a cab home or whatever, have a meal, that sort of thing. It wasn't fair but you couldn't say nothing back, you just enjoyed your football, you just wanted to play football. Black wasn't seen as offensive because it wasn't used. They called us niggers back then, clearly called us niggers. You would hear it in Arsenal, "Those niggers are showing off again." When I went to Tottenham you could see the vibe between the black players and the white players. We were stronger, faster and more skilful but the first thing they would say was, "We don't want none of that flashy football. We want 'give and go.'" If I can receive a ball and beat three or four men, what am I "giving it and going" for?'

Cunningham was released by Arsenal after two years aged sixteen in 1972 with the explanation he was 'not the right material'. Undoubtedly he did not do himself any favours with poor punctuality and his sometimes erratic behaviour; he would often turn up without boots or kit – Johnson often carried a spare pair of socks to lend him – but with both parents working long hours he found it difficult to organise himself and keep to a regular schedule. Arsenal, who had won the 'Double' in 1971, were managed by Bertie Mee and coached by Don Howe, both old school disciplinarians in the English football tradition. Howe was part of the coaching staff for England's 1966 World Cup victory and a stickler for discipline. His Arsenal players personified the professional modern team, well-drilled, strong, effective and a bit dull. The Double winning team were not renowned for their flair but for their efficacy as a unit. Anyone who did not conform to the Arsenal code, on or off the pitch, stood out and risked falling out with management sooner or later.

Cunningham was devastated when Arsenal rejected him. Football had always come easily to him, he was the star in any side he represented and his outstanding athleticism and extraordinary skill marked him out at every level. Now like so many black teenage players it looked as if he had missed his chance and would become just another promising but ultimately unsuccessful footballer. He confided to friends that he did not enjoy the training sessions at Arsenal which were the polar opposite to his style of play; instead of running freely with the ball he was told to pass it as quickly as possible to a more senior player. Bob Cottingham later commented, 'There were some mistakes made at Arsenal. When they played him in trials they always played him out wide on the touchline, but that was not the way I played him because he withered out there. I played him behind the strikers, he did much more damage there, I felt he was isolated somewhat on the wing.' Conforming to a set pattern of play did not suit his temperament as an independent and increasingly confident teenager; he was most comfortable playing football in the instinctive way he always had. But if football did not want him then maybe he did not want it. There was more to life – dancing, music, clothes and girls. London could offer it all to a young lad with spirit and imagination.

2

BLUES & SOUL

By the time Laurie Cunningham had turned sixteen in 1972, the racist jibes he suffered on the football field would have sounded familiar from his experience of growing up on the streets of Finsbury Park. Animosity felt by his peers towards the police and the authorities was universal. Stop and search was a law used specifically against black teenagers as a controlling tactic by the police. In Islington unemployment and homelessness, particularly among school-leavers, were on the increase. Struggling to find a meaningful identity and feeling estranged from their parents' culture, the term 'Black British' was yet to be conceived for this hard-pressed and disorientated younger generation. Overlooked by a society that was not that interested in what they had to say, these disregarded youths were left to fend for themselves. By describing this fractious, formative time, a clear context emerges of what life was like in London for Cunningham and his generation. He went on to become an important, pioneering figure for this group and his later success proved that you could be black, British and achieve at a national and international level regardless of your colour.

Keith Cunningham and Eustus Isiae became best friends at Archway Secondary School. Both were born, and spent their early years, in the Caribbean. Eustus who lived there for his first seven years, recalls the disconnection and anger he felt towards his parents when he was growing up in Islington. If he was stopped by police or his parents received a phone call to say he had been taken to a station for questioning, 'They wouldn't believe you if you said the police had stopped you for no reason, instead they'd beat you and send you to bed. My parents were the ones coming out of slavery … if they were going for a job they'd say "Good morning sir, I've come about the job" but they wouldn't look in the man's face in case he'd say no, you're too rude looking in the man's face,' he recalls. He also remembers the difficulty of being a black school leaver and looking for work. Walking past a shop one day he spotted a sign in the window: 'It said "young lad wanted apply within". So I went inside and said, "I'm applying about the job," and the owner said to a colleague, "Didn't you take that sign down? Sorry about that, it's already gone." So every day I walked past the shop and the sign was still there. Maybe if I was a white boy I'd still not have got the job, but as soon as the man saw me, he just didn't really want to know. That was the sort of thing we were up against.' The amount of young blacks walking the streets and sleeping rough after being thrown out of home or released from the care system at the age of sixteen, when legal responsibility ended for them, rose steadily in the borough. Nowhere existed to cater for their needs until a charismatic former bricklayer from Antigua set about addressing the problem and sought out premises to open a refuge for these vulnerable youths. Herman Edwards founded the Harambee Project, one of the first black hostels, in a derelict property in 1973 on Holloway Road. Harambee – a Swahili word meaning co-operation – came to be better known, locally and more simply, as the Black House. It was set up in a disused butcher's shop and its adjacent buildings. Targeting drifting black youths, it attempted to break the cycle of petty crime, borstal or prison, and further crime that had trapped so many. Brother Herman, as everybody called him, was a rarity for the time – a sympathetic adult who was willing to act as advocate for the hostel's troubled occupants. He prioritised representation of black youths in police stations and magistrates courts, most of whom had ben detained without legal counsel after being arrested under the 'sus' law. The title 'Brother' was an important one as it suggested parity; a more paternalistic title, such as father or mister, would have provoked immediate distrust amongst the wary teenagers in his care.

In an attempt to get behind the alarmist headlines and moral panic about black teenagers, the *Sunday Times Magazine* tasked reporter Peter Gillman and photographer Colin Jones to 'go and find who is doing all the mugging'. Their feature on the Black House, which appeared in September 1973 and spread over eighteen pages, is an extraordinary, shocking and sensitive portrait of daily life at the hostel with Jones's outstanding photographs shining a light on a young and alienated community with little hope. He says of the time he spent there, 'It was very tough, some of them were very sad. It's one of the hardest assignments I have ever done.' After publication he exhibited his photographs to great acclaim at the prestigious Photographers' Gallery in central London. The reality of what he had captured only dawned on him at the opening night when he was asked: 'In which part of America did you take these photographs?' and he replied, 'Holloway Road, about three miles from here.'

When asked if mugging was a common practice, Jones's view is that it was far too risky and the rewards too unpredictable to be worth it – plus any crime against whites carried severe penalties. 'They were great cat burglars, they mainly stole amongst themselves and the reason they did that was that they knew that they wouldn't be split on,' he observes. By quoting the hostel's inhabitants in depth, Gillman's words give voice to a totally marginalised stratum of society. One inhabitant named Paul recounts his experience of growing up in London. At a job interview he was told, 'You don't mind if we call you a black bastard or a wog or a nigger or anything because it's entirely a joke. I told him to keep the job ... When I was small I used to go around saying that I'm English and I'm proud of being English. But then suddenly it hit me that the English didn't want me to be an Englishman. I don't call myself nothing to do with the English race in fact. They look upon me as a stranger so I look upon myself as a stranger in this country.' Another boy, eighteen-year-old Beckford, mentions Enoch Powell's offer of repatriation and says that if he was given his fare and £2,000 he would go back to the Caribbean, and speaks about police use of stop and search: 'Sometimes you get mad and you get nicked for assault – you just push them away and it's assault. They come and put their hand in your pocket. You can't let them do that. Even though they say they have the right to do that. You say you'll turn your pocket out but they say no, they still want to search you. You say no and the fight starts like this and the next day you're in court. Then you get six months or something.'

And Jones recalls one sad and mysterious character who hid himself away in the crowded and often violent house,

'He wouldn't let me near him with a camera even if I paid him. I used to spend a lot of time in his room talking to him because he was interesting, and one day he said to me, "My legs have swollen up," and Herman wasn't there. I had a friend who was a doctor and I asked him to come and have a look at him and he told him, "What you've got is beriberi from lack of vitamins." He'd cook rice and a tin of sardines and he'd overcook it, he cooked any goodness out of it, and that's all he lived on, and that's how he got beriberi. It's a tropical disease really, not many people in London get beriberi. Then one day he'd gone, nobody knew where or why he was there.' More disturbingly he recalls an incident with a boy known as Johnny Rasta who took his frustration with his father to extremes; one day 'He had a big argument with his dad and broke a bottle and put it in his face and blinded his father, and for six months he wouldn't get out of bed, he was in a state of depression over what he'd done.'

Keith Cunningham worked at the Black House and was part of a wide group of friends who passed through its doors. Eustus, whose home life was difficult, often spent the night there if he had argued with his parents. It provided a sense of community and freedom for many young men and women who had nowhere else to go. Edwards brought in teachers to help some of the youths with reading and writing, and invited speakers to come and talk about Afro-Caribbean history. Muhammad Ali even visited once and donated a pair of boxing boots and a signed poster as a gift to the project. 'It was somewhere to go, you could have a game of pool in there, they would teach you about black history, try to get you to see if you could understand. Most of our parents didn't want us to go there because as far as they were concerned we were being told bad things. Our parents were the type that would turn the other cheek if you slapped them. God said it was best to let them slap the other one too,' Eustus recalls.

The most famous celebration of Caribbean identity in London is the Notting Hill Carnival; more than just a street parade, it carries important spiritual and mythological dimensions too. The idea of a whole area being given over to a black festival unsettled the Metropolitan police who suspected many black youths of being inherently criminal. On Bank Holiday Monday 31 August 1976 the carnival descended into a riot with running battles between the police and groups of black youths. 325 police were injured and 68 people were arrested. Described inaccurately as a race riot by some newspapers it was the first riot in a generation directed solely against the police. Organisers complained of the heavy police presence and one carnival goer complained 'all the people in the carnival procession coming down Portobello Road could see was the police cordon – a forest of helmets. It made them angry because it is our carnival, not theirs.' The riot was a fight back by black youths against constant daily harrassment from the police. Stung by criticism of their colleagues in the press, police in Islington patrolled in vans, stopping black teenagers demanding to know if they had been at the carnival.

Eight weeks after the riot, on 26 October, eighteen black teenagers from Islington, between the ages of fourteen and nineteen, were arrested by CID detectives at their homes and workplaces without warrants and held for three days at various police stations in north London. Anxious to get statements before the boys could get any legal advice the police used disorientation tactics and moved them between stations without informing their parents of their whereabouts, until 'confessions' were taken and they were brought before Highbury Magistrates Court and remanded for trial. Two of the accused were staying at the Black House when they were arrested. One of them, Michael Otway, can be seen as sadly typical of the vulnerable young people who ended up there. Born in Grenada he came to England at the age of seven and was expelled from school for fighting aged thirteen after which he was disowned by his parents. Homeless since he was fourteen years old he was advised to go to the Black House by his social worker where he was picked up for burglary by Holloway police and sent to borstal and afterwards returned to the Black House where he was again picked up by police in connection with the Notting Hill charge. The eighteen defendants were remanded for four and a half months from their committal in December to their trial in April 1977, so the police effectively locked them away and removed them from the streets well before they had to answer any charges.

The trial at the Old Bailey lasted for three months (with an extra delay caused by the Queen's Silver Jubilee celebrations). The jury retired for 170 hours and from the questions they asked the judge were clearly uncomfortable with the multiple charges brought before them. Three of the defendants, including two brothers, pleaded guilty in return for a borstal sentence. All the others accused with the charge of 'conspiracy to rob and steal' were found not guilty, neither were any found guilty of charges relating specifically to the

Carnival. The jury had simply found the case too difficult too understand. Crucially the prosecution based its evidence on 'confessions' and none of the fifty-two witnesses called could point to a defendant and say 'that's the man', neither could police photographs produced in court place any of the defendants at the Carnival on the Bank Holiday Monday. The embarrassment and expense of the whole affair completely discredited the 'sus' law which was finally repealed four years later in 1981.

Laurie Cunningham offered his own take on his background when he told a newspaper in 1977, 'I was born a Londoner and an Englishman', but, 'you think back to where your family really belong. My parents and older brother were all born in Jamaica and I've been brought up to think of it as somewhere special. I've never been to Kingston but I feel that I know it all from the pictures I've been shown of the place and the stories I've heard.' He goes on to query the surnames of his extended family such as Cunningham, Laing and McGibbon – the names of Scottish slave masters – and comments with quiet irony, 'You do think back to where your family really belong, and wonder which part of Africa, or which tribe your great, great, great, great grandfather might have come from. I suppose we could go back to African names but because we've been civilised we've got good old Scottish names and we are Cunninghams.'

Edwards attempted to cultivate a confidence in his charges, or as he put it a 'sure footing'. Let down by the education system, he felt they needed to learn their own history before they could advance. Brought up on a borrowed English culture and rejecting their parents acquiescent values, they had no real sense of who they were so expressed their frustration by rebelling against society through crime and violence. He concluded, 'They are empty people, people without any ingredients of their own society. They have to understand they are black. I think this is the greatest complex young people have in this country. Harambee is a project to let you know you are black. It's a project to let you know that white society doesn't understand you and it's best when you understand yourself, because then you can participate in white society.' One rare sympathetic policeman, Inspector Williams, from Upper Street station, who had previously spent time in Jamaica and visited the Black House regularly, remarked of the place, 'Harambee is the only hope for some of these young kids. They have rejected the society in which we live and it's the only place where you can attempt to get them back into society again. Some of the officers regard it as a den of thieves. But the people in there do not exist because of Harambee. Harambee exists because of them, and there's nowhere else for many of them to go.'

In the tense, sometimes aggressive environment, a certain tolerant chaos existed and Edwards was criticised for the lack of structure in the house by visiting social workers and local authority inspectors. Islington Council never fully trusted his financial management or the fact that he had no formal qualifications. In 1977 he was prosecuted when auditors checked his books and found evidence of unauthorised expenditure for visiting courts and prison. Although the presiding judge accepted he had spent none of the money on himself he was sentenced to six months in Pentonville prison and when funding was withdrawn the Black House closed its doors and the derelict buildings were demolished soon after. Colin Jones remembers Edwards in the following way, 'He worked hard under the most extreme conditions, finding time at any hour for the people in his care. One of the many things Herman did was to try and get bail for those who had been arrested and charged, keeping them out of prison for as long as possible, especially if it was a first offence. For an ex-bricklayer he made a pretty good social worker.'

Having spent the early years of his life in Jamaica Keith Cunningham identified strongly with the so-called 'rebel generation' that allied itself with reggae music in the 1970s – a generation with an awareness of the teachings of Marcus Garvey and Martin Luther King that asserted independence of thought and cultural expression as crucial to the development and survival of the black race – and whose social gatherings at sound system and blues parties were an essential part of this identity. By contrast his brother was a London-born soul boy or 'West End man', who danced to a different beat. 'I was a bopper and he was a swinger,' he explains. Through his involvement in football Cunningham became immersed in British culture to a much greater degree than his older brother did. Where Laurie loved soul music Keith was a reggae man all the way. Reggae was defiantly working-class and had a powerful Rastafarian ideology of simplicity and spirituality. Soul on the other hand was largely apolitical and concerned itself with sophistication and personal aspiration, two more overtly Western traits.

Attending twice-weekly training sessions at Arsenal, Cunningham picked up more than just football skills and began to dress like the older players he admired. The footballer style was set by the likes of Chelsea in London at this time and was a smart and casual look. Button-down Ben Sherman shirts were worn with pressed trousers, cardigans and loafers: versatile outfits that were smart enough to be worn straight from training to a party or club. Cunningham's school friend Robert Johnson remembers being influenced by this look and recalls shopping at a men's outfitters on Farringdon Road that specialised in Ben Sherman shirts. He had parallel trousers made to measure by a friend's father who was a tailor on Green Lanes in Haringey – 'straight down, sharp' – and says, 'you would do anything to play for the club, so you had to look the part too.' As they grew to young adults the Cunningham brothers followed separate lifestyles and kept different hours. Keith followed a Jamaican routine, where the night's entertainment began around midnight and between clubs and house parties would continue until the following morning many hours later, at which time his brother would be getting ready to go to football training.

Despite the harshness and discrimination of everyday life – or perhaps because of it – black music and fashion in London underwent a productive, creative phase during this time. One tangible expression of identity was through music. A group of boys from the Black House, including Eustus and Keith, established a sound system called 'Sir Power, the Killer Sound', that played every Friday night at Archway Methodist Hall. Keith came up with the name after buying a 1,000-watt amp from Muzic City in Finsbury Park – stockist of some of the best electrical equipment around. With the rallying call of 'Sir Power on the Hour', at its height it attracted six to seven hundred revellers to its dances. Running a 'sound' was a serious enterprise, you needed an electrical engineer, a sound engineer who knew about speakers and amplification, someone who knew how to produce the distinctive bass line – and reliable transportation. Sir Power built a good reputation playing house parties and town halls in Hornsey and Finsbury Park, against the dominant north London sound systems of the day such as Fatman Sound in Tottenham. Eustus explains, 'If people were keeping a dance they'd put us on the bill because we were up-and-coming, our crowd would come and pay their fifty pences, we used to play West Green Road in Tottenham, clash with Fatman sound. Chicken sound in Stoke Newington at St Mark's Rise – he was famous because his dance used to go on until two in the afternoon.' Records were sent directly to Eustus from Jamaica by Prince Buster's record shop at 127 Orange Street in Kingston, weeks before they received a UK release date. Giant speaker cabinets were made by a friend's father who was a carpenter and the local greengrocer Mr Young lent them his van to help ferry equipment around. On one occasion a police van was made available by Inspector Williams to get Sir Power to a dance on time. With a crowd waiting outside the hall in Archway, and to ease congestion, a 'Black Maria' was sent to pick them up and transport equipment to the venue. 'It made a change, usually they were confiscating it!' Keith remarks.

Any sound system worth its salt had to be innovative and stay a step ahead of its competitors by playing exclusive tracks that could not be heard anywhere else. These specials or 'dubplates' were cut by a producer in the studio as one-off versions of a song, often with effects added on especially for sound systems. Eustus recalls a piece of good fortune when they got one over on a rival, more established, sound: 'we cut specials in a studio off Old Street run by Clancy Collins, who made dubplates for a sound called Count Shelley, but Shelley never paid him, kept fobbing him off, gave him a few quid here, a few quid there. One day when we were due to play against Shelley, Clancy said to us come down to the studio as he is going to cut some dubs of the dubs. So what Shelley played on the night, we had a different version of it, a dub of the dub. When Shelley played his and said "dubwise from Count Shelley", I'd be on the other side saying "that's not dubwise – anybody can play that" and play the same tune back to him, "but listen to a dubwise from Sir Power", and we'd play a version. He didn't know that Collins had given us all this stuff to mess him up, cos he wouldn't pay him.'

While Keith was preoccupied with reggae his younger brother started to discover the soul scene where he met Bert Jordine when they were teenagers and they quickly became close friends. The two hit it off immediately and it's easy to see why. Jordine is an easy-going affable person. Both shared a similar sense of humour and a mutual interest in fitness and dance. Jordine, born in 1955, was not a footballer but loved martial arts and together they would train in his front room in Tottenham, with his cousin a third Dan karate master. Karate helped with Cunningham's all-round fitness and suppleness on the football field, but also benefited the mental side of his game as he began to develop a calm, meditative routine before matches. Of similar build and height, Jordine would accompany Cunningham to a tailor's shop in Stratford where the pair ordered matching outfits: getting identically cut suits in different colours which they shared with each other. Dressing up to go out became an important part of the evening and trying on different looks was all part of the fun. Jordine cackles with laughter when shown a picture dating from 1979 of Cunningham at London Airport on his way to Spain looking every inch the dapper international footballer saying, 'He's got my shoes on, they were mine and he never gave them back. I've got to get a copy of this.' Then adding, 'We were having suits made all the time, you picked out your material, had the jacket lined; we used to interchange – if I had one in white he'd have one in black and vice versa. We used to buy our shoes in the West End, flat ones for dancing not platforms like most people were wearing. We liked Fred Astaire and Gene Kelly too, we liked their clothes, and even the dances, we copied some of their moves.'

Soul music was riding high in the pop charts by the early 1970s. The music was melodic and well-produced, often with strings added, and squarely aimed at the mass-market. For the soul boys the Motown sound was appreciated but far too ready-made and commercial for their liking. What they sought was something harder and more driven, and they found it in the music of James Brown. His music was raw and primal and urged the listener to dance. Brown's appearance at East Ham Odeon in 1969 was a revelation to all those who witnessed it. The combination of live performance, power and energy and in particular his sliding dance moves left a deep impression. His sharp Ivy League style inspired a memorable look for the soul boys to emulate.

Cunningham's school friend Robert Johnson, primarily a reggae fan, recalls the energy of the time. In Tottenham,

Stoke Newington and Hackney, groups would go to a club, move on to a party and meet again later at a sound system. The possibilities seemed endless and wherever you went you were sure to bump into someone you knew. He recounts a scam he and Cunningham devised to trick their way into the All Nations club, a multistoreyed nightclub in London Fields, Hackney. With no money between them but plenty of determination, they sprinkled themselves with water and approached the doorman saying they had just popped out from the packed club to get some air, to prove it they were drenched in sweat. It was a neat trick but limited, when they tried it a second time they were recognised and refused entry again. Dancing was all anybody wanted to do; sometimes it would be all boys together, other times boys and girls, the circle was tight but inclusive. 'People assumed we were all Jamaican but we weren't, there were people from Antigua, Trinidad – but because it was a mainly Jamaican crowd, it was assumed everyone was from there, but we all just blended,' says Johnson.

When not playing football Cunningham thrived in this glamorous world. Dancing and looking sharp came as naturally to him as kicking a ball and the soul boy world offered him joyful release. His suppleness and athletic ability served him well on the dance floor. To rank as a top dancer you had to be committed enough to see off the competition three, four, or even five times a week and Cunningham spent as much time practising his routines as he did on the training field. A large part of his free time was spent devising and refining set pieces with Jordine. If he liked a particular track he spent days listening to it until he knew it inside out – learning where it stopped and started, how the music progressed and where the instrumental break came in – until he was in tune with the flow of the record.

The place where music, fashion and dance came together was a nondescript club on Wardour Street in Soho called Crackers. The musician Jazzie B of Soul II Soul says of it, 'Crackers was the start of it all with people dancing to the right music in the right atmosphere, and most importantly with the right people. Everyone, all the black guys who were real on the scene were going to Crackers.' It opened its doors in 1973 with a sharp-dressed DJ from Southend called Mark Roman. He played import-only American soul and funk and quickly found a loyal and committed young black audience. At this time West End clubs exercised a quota system for blacks and the few who made it into a club were often frowned upon as sell-outs or court jesters by fellow blacks. With a dearth of credible venues in the West End it was difficult for DJs to attract a regular crowd, so when Crackers started to purely play soul music, first on Tuesday and Friday nights, there was nothing else like it. Owned by the pub chain Wheatley Taverns, who were struggling in a time of recession, Roman's popularity led to him being offered the extra but unpromising time slot of Friday lunchtime, between 12 noon and 2.30 p.m. He took the opportunity to try out new ideas and began playing less obvious music, such as instrumental album tracks and lesser-known B-sides that had caught his ear. Immediately, helped by an admission fee of fifty pence, the session began to attract a very young crowd aged between fifteen and twenty-one – Jazzie B remembers going there as a thirteen-year-old – many of whom were still at school or had recently left to work in shops and junior office jobs. At Crackers, Cunningham found a couple of hours pure escapism in the heart of the West End amidst the clapped-out pubs and dive bars. The club was typical of the locale – unglamorous and shabby from the outside, it struggled to distinguish itself from its neighbours, as it sat dully at 203 Wardour Street. The tired fascia promised a 'Piano and American Rock Bar', while the peeling exterior paintwork was complemented by a careworn interior. Once inside guests descended to a dimly lit basement with a tiny dance floor edged by a threadbare carpet and serviced by a mercurial PA system that often blew its own speakers. At a push, the club held around five hundred people. In order to stay the right side of the licensing laws customers were given a meal ticket upon entry, to be handed over when ordering drinks in exchange for a mysterious stew. If the management thought they were going to make money from alcohol sales they were mistaken. The teenagers were not interested in lunchtime boozing, they had come for something else, something that made the place different and exciting: a perfect storm of music, dance and atmosphere that was unlike anywhere else in London. Here the best, most dedicated dancers gathered to compete against each other to the newest and most uplifting sounds direct from America. Like other club owners Wheatley Taverns initially barred large groups of blacks from entering, but once the doormen got to know the dancers they soon realised they would help fill the club and it didn't take long for a black audience to dominate.

The prestige in which the dancers were held meant a kind of club within a club existed, as both DJ and dancers pushed the music further in a mutually beneficial relationship. A scene quickly developed by word-of-mouth, without advertising or air-play, until within the space of a few short months it became a rite of passage to go there at least once. In the school playground working-class white boys may have bragged about how many pints they drank at the weekend but their black counterparts could boast 'I went to Crackers', even if they had only stood and queued up outside. The lunchtime session was where the top dancers held court and they soon became as big an attraction as the music. A motley collection of soul boys, skiving schoolchildren and young shopworkers filled the room to shuffle, gape and wonder at the dancing and – in an age when weekly wages came in Manila envelopes – the lure of Crackers with a week's pay fresh in your back pocket proved too strong for many to resist.

In 1976 Mark Roman was replaced by George Power and the music became jazzier as he introduced tracks by artists such as Roy Ayers, Lonnie Liston Smith, Gil Scott-Heron and Airto Moreira and Flora Purim. The blend of funk and improvisation shifted the music towards the fusion style known as jazz-funk. Power realised that the relationship between the dancers and himself was the key to success. To increase rivalry he arranged dance contests, or burn-ups, with a cash prize for the winner which Cunningham sometimes entered. As part of the chosen few, Cunningham and Jordine were supplied with advance mix tapes to practise and refine their routines. They often danced together and must have been a beguiling sight to onlookers in their tailored, coordinated suits, one in black, the other in white as they moved across the floor. As friends they were inseparable, if you saw one, you saw the other, and the easy-going bond that existed between them was noticeable for everyone to see. Jordine comments on the style of dancing he and Cunningham favoured: 'It was freestyle, it was just expression in the moment. He could do the spins and we used to love the jazz dancers and take moves from them. We had crowds round us when we danced, we'd get soaking wet from dancing and have a change of clothes in the car.'

None but the most confident approached the floor when the top men were on it as a challenge would be thrown down the moment anyone stepped off the perimeter carpet. A dance-off could develop spontaneously or be more formally staged – but once it began the crowd parted and protocol took over. The dancers were mostly second-generation British Jamaicans with a sizeable contingent coming from east London. One of the top dancers from that part of town was Dez Parkes. He grew up listening to reggae but as he got older started to look beyond it and by 1973 was exploring the West End. At the Whisky-A-Go-Go on Wardour Street he saw American GIs dancing to the latest funk in a way he had not seen before, twisting and contorting to the groove. He was hooked and began to copy them. He remarks, 'All of that style came from the speakeasys, the clubs in Harlem, the slickness of the dance entertainment is where it came from, it's all in the heritage', and adds, 'You were looked at as stepping outside of your culture by reggae people. All Jamaicans were reggae first, it was your first port of call. Then we realised it was a specialist scene, so we stepped out of it; we wanted to do something different, there was a sense of freedom. We wanted to dance and look good. People, black and white, were starting to integrate'. He asserts that black dancers were the pioneers for the sucessful club DJs and promoters of today but feels they have not been given credit for it. 'We had to fight the wars for them to walk the streets today. The black community could only meet in churches, community halls and shebeens back then. We created something but we haven't been recognised, we are just a commodity. The London soul scene – a lot of creative thinkers came out of that – we had to create our own survival.'

He describes the dancing style as follows: 'Black dancing is about moving your hips and your waist fluently, it is almost like you are a snake. First and foremost you are dancing to the beat regardless of the tempo; when you're dancing you're dancing at all times to the drum so you're not out of sync. You are meant to be making a picture, telling a story. We were known as boogie dancers as opposed to jazz dancers – we were more free-flowing dancers. However I used to do some of the moves the Nicholas Brothers did, kick turns, barrel turns, the splits, that's jazz dancing. Laurie Cunningham was doing it too, there were so many moves.' And he describes how the dance-offs worked: 'We would have a wide circle and two dancers would battle within it. A track would be picked by one of them and they both would dance off to that. Then they would play the other track, so it was two rounds. It was a rhythmic war. Some people had their special track that they danced to and they could do their best dance to it, so that was in their favour. The trick was if you could take that guy's track and his moves and throw it back in his face, then you do your style and he would have to try and combat you. Nine out of ten times it wouldn't happen if you were a really good dancer, because you would be able to do what he does but do it better, and then go into your flow and he was lost, he'd have to walk off the floor to boos. Whoever the crowd had thought won it, they let them know. If you lost it wasn't like you lost face, it was just the best man won on the night. It would make you a better dancer, you could win one night but get your arse whopped five other nights of the week, so what happened was you'd go home, work on the things you weren't too sharp on and you'd add more to your repertoire by working out moves and within that you'd be finding your own style.'

After a winner had been declared the gladiatorial mood dissipated and the dance floor returned to normal as a more relaxed atmosphere returned. On arriving at the club Jordine, the more talkative of the two friends, would approach Power to ask him 'what's happening George?' to find out what he had lined up for them or ask 'where are we going?' to see where else he was playing that week. With a mixtape in the car stereo the pair travelled to out of the way venues such as Scamps in Hemel Hempstead for the 'George Power Soul Night', where they showcased the moves they had been working on all week. Back in Crackers, Power used Cunningham and Jordine's skill as dance partners to break new records, knowing they could help to get a track a positive response from the elitist crowd, who determined a record's popularity in seconds flat, or ignored it with such disdain that it never saw the light of day again. The early seventies fad for martial arts was also an influence as the vogue for Kung Fu films found its way on to the dance floor as the quick, flashing movements of the actors were imitated and reproduced. Cunningham and Jordine both practised karate and the harmonising of mind and body appealed to Cunningham's enquiring mind. The Hong Kong films that played regularly as double bills in West End cinemas were full of ingenious stunts that caught the imagination of a whole generation of British youth and echoed the craze for spaghetti westerns a few years earlier that had resonated so strongly with the Jamaican reggae audience. Although dance-off's were serious business there was room for a lighter side too. One of the best dancers, Leon Herbert, was noted for the old man moves he threw into a routine for the sheer fun of it after seeing the Jackie Chan film *Drunken Master*. The appeal of Kung Fu films lay in the athleticism and panache of the lead performers and the stylised spins and rolls they employed could be cleverly adapted to dancing. With his heroes Bruce Lee and Fred Astaire in the forefront of his mind, Cunningham would interpret the gestures he had seen on screen. A friend recalls watching him in full flow: 'He did Bruce Lee moves on the floor, bang! His leg would flick out and hold it for a second and move on, it was like dancing with a storyboard. Laurie would practise all hours in his house so it looked like everything was off the cuff but there was a lot of thought behind it as well.'

By the long hot summer of 1976 Crackers popularity was at its peak and the Friday lunchtime session was attracting hundreds of people. For Cunningham, being the centre of attention was essential; he loved the recognition and the limelight and being admired for his moves and the cut of his clothes. The allure of the best dancers left a powerful impression on the young crowd: 'It was about individuality, sexuality, but it wasn't a premeditated thing, the currency was the dance moves and the clothes and what you looked like, with that currency you got the girls,' remarks Don Letts who danced on the scene as a teenager. The soul clubs signposted the multicultural direction the country was headed. For a generation of black and white teenagers who had grown up and gone to school together, going to a soul club was an extension of the London they all knew. Don Letts states, 'It was an across the board mix, I can't tell you how mixed it was. Categorically, no scene has been as mixed as the soul scene, never ever, before or after, there was a common ground.'

The soul scene was generally ignored by the music press. The one magazine that covered the music was *Blues & Soul* which was important for its chart that listed the latest tracks available from its record outlet Contempo, a cramped upstairs room above a Spanish bar on Hanway Street, an atmospheric side street that connects Oxford Street and Tottenham Court Road. DJs scanned the chart to see what was coming in and pinned up track listings to tell people what they were playing thereby creating instant demand among the crowd. Contempo became an informal meeting place for soul fans and, being a short walk from Crackers, this part of the West End became a hot-spot for anybody interested in the latest music. It was the only place where you could buy singles at the same time as America, at a time when records could take months to get a UK release date. Imports, sold fresh out of the boxes, often without being listened to first were bought on the strength of the label or the artist's name alone and sold out within hours. Shambolic queues formed up the staircase on Thursday, delivery day, and it was on the landing while waiting to be served that many people developed lasting friendships.

In north London a strong teenage dance contingent gravitated to a well-established club called Bluesville in Wood Green. It was owned by Ron Lesley and his Italian wife Nanda. Lesley was a jazz fan with close links to Alexis Korner and the west London blues scene. He had opened his club in the 1950s as a Trad Jazz and Blues venue where Eric Clapton and Led Zeppelin had played in the early days of their careers but by the 1970s the music tilted more towards soul and reggae and it evolved into a kind of ad-hoc cultural centre for local black youths that hosted live performances, dance competitions and film screenings. For keen young dancers, Bluesville, a few miles north of Cunningham's home in Finsbury Park, was a place where you could find out how good a dancer you really were. Steve Salvari was part of a north London posse that always 'came correct' and remembers Cunningham from those days. He says he was quiet but 'extrovert in his dancing. Him and Bert could move about a bit. He looked up to us and that was one of the things that made him really popular among us'. He was not afraid to take on his peers either, Salvari says. 'He did challenge me once; I saw him off though, he didn't do it twice!' If a well-known dancer was due to visit a huge buzz went round the area.

A dancer with one of the biggest reputations was Leon Herbert from Islington. When word got out that he was coming to Bluesville local dancers eagerly upped their game in readiness for the challenge. Salvari practised hard until he felt confident he had a chance of victory but remembers being taught a lesson come the night. 'All the guys turned up to challenge him. We were there in our tank-tops and Ravel shoes doing Jackson 5 kind of moves. Leon turned up in a double-breasted suit, patent leather shoes, a clutch bag and a shirt and tie. We had lost before we'd even begun. When he started dancing he was doing ballet and tap moves.' For Herbert himself, Bluesville offered a release from the pressures of everyday life in London, which he describes as 'extremely racist, very racist, but in Bluesville it didn't matter. Music was all we had, you lived and died for it.'

Herbert earned the mantle of top dancer while still in his teens and drew a crowd wherever he performed. His interest in clothes led him to the King's Road in Chelsea and introduced him to a colourful and outlandish *beau-monde* of clandestine clubs and parties. Some of the best dance music was found in the gay clubs and bars around the King's Road. At a time when the majority of clubs did not allow blacks in the door, gay clubs provided an environment where dancers could freely express themselves without being gawped at by nervous white onlookers and were an entry point to a world of fashion and celebrity. Herbert was invited to a hideaway club in Kensington named El Sombrero, which had the distinction of being the first club in London to have coloured lighting beneath its glass floor, and discovered an exclusive and fantastical world once inside the door. 'The way people dressed was amazing. I saw a guy in riding boots and jodhpurs and he looked really cool, this was high, high fashion, this was completely new and now came a completely different kind of music. I'd come from heavy funk but now I'm hearing Barry White. This was lighter music and the only place they played this kind of music was gay clubs and they used to play funky jazz too which I'd never heard before.' One particular track, *Fantasy* by Johnny Hammond, with its complex yet subtle and lilting instrumentation had an instant impact. 'When I heard this and saw those guys dancing I was thinking what the hell are they doing? The dance is completely different, they are dancing on their toes. The whole night I just watched, then I copied them and turned it into my thing. They are thinking they are picking me up but I'm learning the moves, now my dancing has changed, it's lighter, I'm on the balls of my feet.'

Ronnie Scott's in Soho, the jewel in the crown of British jazz clubs, became home to a dancing elite every Thursday night. The upstairs room where black dancers gathered was more exclusive (and pricier) than most other clubs in the West End. Leon Herbert and Dez Parkes danced there and Jordine recalls that when he and Cunningham went, after paying the entrance fee they 'had enough money for one drink and a bag of chips on the way home'. It was a dancers' heaven that stripped away any fripperies and fashions and focused purely on the best contemporary jazz music. The upstairs room was the place a dancer aspired to once he had put in the hours at Crackers or Bluesville and developed a unique style of his own. Jordine was a confirmed jazz fan by then and spent his money on expensive import albums. Both he and Cunningham loved the sophistication of the music and the special atmosphere inside the room transported them to an exhilarating place more like New York or Paris than London. Like all good dancers they were sponges and could copy the moves they saw and adapt them for their own use.

By the mid-1970s London dancers were at the cutting edge of music and style. In a photograph from around 1976 taken while he is out clothes shopping, Cunningham looks good in his soul boy garb. He wears a pair of bespoke 'pegs', the pleated baggy trousers inspired by 1940s tailoring. For the trousers to hang right he had to find the correct weight of material. Cunningham chose a heavy-looking flannel with a high waist that looks great paired with a more contemporary tight-fitting leather bomber jacket. At a time when flared trousers and patchwork denim had come to dominate men's fashion, Cunningham's look is pared down and eye-catching. His short hair, with a grown-out razor parting visible, referencing the black GI haircuts of the Second World War, would also have been unusual at a time when Afro hairstyles, like long hair, were everywhere. Most significantly he is wearing flat-soled co-respondent shoes that were perfect for dancing. It is a unique look with a street feel. Put together with care and subtlety it shows that he was way ahead of the pack when it came to looking good.

In the London Laurie Cunningham grew up in where racism was rife, dancing was more than just escapism, it helped to define who you were.' The soul boys were the advance guard for a generation of black Britons who did things on their own terms. Frustrated at how they were treated, barred from nightclubs because of their colour and stopped from walking freely down the streets by the police, these teenagers responded by creating a culture of their own. The version of Britain they kept in their heads was a graceful and elegant one where the way you dressed and the way you danced signified an approach to life that was markedly different to the grey reality.

3

LAND OF THE RISING SON

Clapton Orient football club was founded in Hackney in 1881 and changed its name to Leyton Orient after the Second World War. The club moved further east across Hackney Marshes to its present home at Brisbane Road in Leyton in 1937. This once marshy, riverine land at the bottom of the Lea Valley was an unpromising place to situate a football ground, prone to flooding and suffering from poor drainage. The pitch at Brisbane Road, which has the River Lea running beneath it, was heavy and muddy, and at one low point in the 1970s so badly waterlogged it became unusable for three months. Long-suffering supporters took a perverse pride in the often appalling state of the pitch, which encouraged the more physical style of football to be played. By the time Laurie Cunningham arrived, the club had spent many years in the lower reaches of the Football League but had earned a reputation for being one of the more friendly clubs in London.

This was in no small part due to the large local Jewish following that had grown around the club, and a charismatic and loyal chairman called Harry Zussman. A well-fed, cigar-chomping East End shoe manufacturer, Zussman ran the club for over thirty years from 1949 until his death in 1981. In the mid-1960s he brought in unlikely glamour when he persuaded two business associates, Bernard Delfont and Leslie Grade, to invest in the club and join the board as directors. Grade and his brother Lew were the leading talent and theatrical agents in London who also ran the ATV television company. Delfont controlled a stable of West End theatres and could be seen every year on the red carpet welcoming Her Majesty the Queen to the London Palladium for the Royal Variety Performance.

Zussman employed his own unique brand of showmanship in the dressing room after games by rewarding players with notes pulled from a large wad or offering complimentary tickets to his partner's West End shows. When the club relocated in the 1930s the original Jewish East End around Whitechapel was starting to spread to the less crowded and airier northern and eastern suburbs of London. A generation had begun to make its way in the world and moved on to places like Finchley and Hendon in the north and Leyton and Stratford in the east. Leyton Orient, a small, close-knit club offered a welcome that its bigger, more famous neighbour West Ham United did not – whose core support was drawn primarily from white working-class dock workers. Zussman loved to trade on the club's underdog status in the area and generated a good-humoured 'them and us' mentality which held a strong appeal to the Jewish psyche. This liberal, everyone-welcome atmosphere proved attractive to a dedicated band of Jewish supporters despite the limitations often evident on the pitch.

After the shock of rejection from Arsenal, Cunningham might easily have turned his back on football but Bob Cottingham was convinced he could get him into a London club and set about using his contacts to find him one. He was friendly with a former professional player whose son had graduated from Highgate North Hill to Arsenal alongside Cunningham. That boy, Glenn Roeder, went on to play professionally for Queens Park Rangers and managed both West Ham United and Newcastle United. Roeder senior would often drive the two boys to training at Arsenal's Highbury Stadium and take them to away fixtures. Glenn Roeder, a talented ball-playing defender, was released by Arsenal at the same time as Cunningham and his father immediately contacted an old teammate from his playing days to see if he could offer his boy a second chance at a new club.

George Petchey became the manager of Second Division Leyton Orient in 1971. A tough ex-professional from Whitechapel who had played wing half (defensive midfield) for West Ham and Brighton in the days 'when centre half's had cut heads and broken collar bones', he was keen to change the traditional, physical playing style at the club to a more thoughtful, dynamic one. His assistant was Arthur Rowe, the former Tottenham Hotspur manager who had devised the 'push and run' style of football at White Hart Lane after the war. Push and run was a high-tempo attacking style of football that encouraged players to move position often and take on greater responsibility for the ball. Used with fluidity and pace it had earned Tottenham their first ever league title in 1951. For it to work effectively, push and run needed intelligent players with a good touch and the awareness and vision to play the right pass at the right time – attributes that Cunningham and Roeder both possessed. Petchey agreed to see Roeder for a trial and when told by his father that Arsenal 'don't half let some good players go', was curious enough to ask who else he had in mind. He suggested Cunningham, adding 'he's a bit of a rascal, a bit of an awkward boy', to which Petchey responded 'get him here, let's talk to him'. Petchey, now in his eighties, looks a diminutive, domestic figure in his carpet slippers, sipping tea in his small comfortable living room just outside Brighton, with his wife Moll providing generous plates of sandwiches – but it is not difficult to picture him years ago at Leyton Orient shouting, cajoling and berating his players to do things his way. He has a natural authority and calmly expressed knowledge, to which young players must have responded.

Laurie Cunningham did, after a difficult start. Orient teammate Bobby Fisher, a sixteen-year-old apprentice at the time, remembers the morning of Cunningham's trial: 'The arrangement was to be at the ground for 9.30 so we could go to training. So we got changed, no Laurie. We warmed up for another fifteen minutes, no Laurie, and by 10.30 still no Laurie. George started picking the sides and I look across at this shadowy figure just casually walking across the pitches to us. You could see it was a black guy, as there weren't many black guys around. I thought it must be him. The first thing I thought to myself was this guy has been let go by Arsenal and Orient have given him a chance and it's probably his last chance of getting into the professional game. If I was him I'd be sprinting across the pitch and grovelling on my hands and knees, but this guy just sauntered across the pitch and just stood there and didn't say a word.'

When asked why he was so late, he replied, 'I overslept.' What sounded like arrogance – punctuality was a perennial problem – would become more understandable as Petchey patiently spent time getting to know the boy and gradually drew him out of himself. After such an inauspicious start Cunningham had a lot to prove and started to do so right away. Petchey recalls: 'I stuck him into a training match without introducing him to anyone and he was brilliant. When I say brilliant I mean he did a lot of things that you wouldn't expect a kid to do. He went past the full back and he looked up and we had a centre forward who was big, and he just plonked it on his head. I was sitting with Arthur Rowe on the touchline, and I looked at Arthur and he looked at me and said "I've had great players but I've never seen anybody do that." He must have done it five times, went down the line, crossed it and it went exactly where he wanted it to go, didn't miss a pass all day. We had four or five wingers who went down the line and crossed it and it hit the full back in the face or on the body, so we'd never get a decent cross from them. But Laurie, different class. He would swerve it round the full back and he'd put it where he wanted to put it every time. That was his talent. There was nothing he couldn't do. He could do anything once you gave him the ball, he loved playing with the ball. I said I'd sign him.'

Cunningham's athleticism and running off the ball were a gift for a manager trying to mould his team into an elegant push-and-run side. Frustratingly for Petchey too many of his players were content to whack the ball the length of the pitch while doggedly holding their position. Excited by the teenage prospect but conscious that he needed careful handling, Petchey deputised Fisher to keep a watchful eye on the new arrival. Fisher was Orient through and through. Mixed-race with an Afro hairstyle and striking light grey eyes, he had been adopted as a baby by a local Jewish family named Lazarus with strong connections to the club. Mark Lazarus was a notable former Orient player and his sister Rosie had brought up the infant Fisher. Cunningham noted the relaxed, liberal feel of the club which allowed Petchey to be innovative and to offer local young black players a chance. After he joined, Orient could count five black players on their books. Fisher comments on the mentoring role he was given by Petchey: 'He wanted me to push these guys, to filter them in. I was the senior black player aged sixteen! I was there to slow Laurie down a bit, make sure he was there on time and say to him, "I know you want to do your own thing but sometimes you have to play the game a little bit because you may be under pressure if you don't."'

Later, when Cunningham and Fisher broke into the first team, Petchey was heavily criticised by the local press and wider community for fielding so many non-whites. By this time he had also signed the Indian-born player Ricky Heppolette, a strong midfielder, for the specific purpose of protecting Cunningham on the pitch, and the skilful and aggressive young striker John Chiedoze, a refugee from the Biafra–Nigeria civil war. Supporters of the National Front wrote regularly telling him he should stop playing 'these niggers' and he remembers falling out with a local sports reporter who could not understand why he was signing so many blacks to the club. The fact that Bobby Fisher was mixed-race and brought up by a Jewish family didn't seem to make much difference either. He put it bluntly: 'In those days if you had a suntan you were counted as black.' Petchey responded to his critics by inviting them to watch a local school match where he assured them they would soon discover that the best players were all black. To the local reporter's charge that his black players lacked courage and were cowardly, a depressingly common view held throughout football, he responded: 'You tell me Muhammad Ali is a coward. I say no, I don't believe that. I tell you what, three of them will be great players. Laurie Cunningham will be the best, then John Chiedoze behind him and Bobby Fisher.'

Cunningham was signed as an apprentice by Leyton Orient in August 1972 aged sixteen and made his first team debut two years later in August 1974. Orient were assembling a good footballing side under Petchey and by the final months of the 1973–74 season were vying for promotion to the First Division for only the second time in their history. With the top three teams automatically promoted, Orient lay fourth and needed to win their last game – played at home in May 1974 versus Aston Villa – to secure two points and a guaranteed promotion spot. But for all their reputation as a friendly club with an apparent bonhomie that extended from the boardroom to the playing staff, Orient seemed content to stay within the limited horizons of a small London club. Petchey bitterly recalls the myopia and lack of ambition he experienced from the board and reveals an insight into how, back then, clubs like Orient were run as personal fiefdoms by the chairmen and members of the board. Knowing his side were capable of winning promotion, Petchey approached his chairman Harry Zussman about the possibility of buying Aston Villa player Ray Graydon to consolidate his team.

'I had often gone into a board meeting and been told to leave because I had asked for money to buy a player. They'd say, "No, we will talk about the money, we don't need you in the boardroom." So they used to kick me out and I would go home. So the next day nothing would be said and I would ask "Did I get any money to spend?" ... There was one particular time when we needed a couple of points to go up to the First Division and we were playing Aston Villa, and the outside right of Aston Villa [Ray Graydon] I had wanted to buy about six weeks before we played them, and Zussman said, "No, we can't give you the money". It was something like £7,000 – bloody nothing. I said, "Do you want to go up or not?" He said, "George, you've done well, you're a good manager, but we don't want to go in the First Division." I said, "You don't want to go in the First Division? What do you think I'm killing myself, and the players are killing themselves for?" He said, "We will only come down again." I gave up in my own mind that day. So I didn't get the money and we drew 1–1 with Aston Villa and that bastard [Graydon] scored a penalty.'

Petchey had debated whether or not to play Cunningham in that crucial match but decided against it, relying on experience and perhaps showing loyalty to the side that had done so well to get within touching distance of the top flight. He also knew that the club were not going to match his ambition and that he would be forced to rely on the squad of players he had already assembled. It was unsurprising, then, when Cunningham made his first team debut at the start of the following season. Petchey had calculated that if he could get hold of a player who was in the top forty in London he would be able to build the team around such an individual. In the young Laurie Cunningham he was sure he had found that man. The two years Petchey spent nurturing Cunningham had not been easy. As he had shown on the day of his trial, punctuality and responding to discipline meant little to the young player. On the one occasion that Petchey spoke to his father Elias on the telephone he had been told, 'He needs some looking after because he has had a free run, because I've been working. Don't be frightened to do whatever you want with him, because that's what he needs.' He soon came up against a defensive, self-contained young man used to living on his wits. Unlike many of his peers Cunningham did not come from a strong footballing background. His father considered the game to be little more than a pastime, like cricket, to be played at your leisure. Petchey realised early on that he had constantly to speak to Cunningham to slowly earn his trust, and once he understood what his manager could do for him Cunningham began to open up, and a bond developed between the two men.

Fisher believes the understanding shown by Petchey came at exactly the right time and suggests that without it Cunningham could easily have drifted away from the game. With an exceptional talent he nonetheless still had much to learn, and a nurturing, holistic approach was the surest way to get the best out of the gifted but raw teenager. Petchey remembers with wry exasperation now, but deep frustration at the time, the lengths he was forced to go to with his young player: 'His idea of playing football was playing on a Saturday then having a great time all week, then coming in and playing again Saturday. He thought he could do it like that. Gradually he learnt. He was such a bugger not turning up on time. I remember I fined him twice a week for six weeks for lateness. I said right, I'm going to fine you £10 every time you are late.

First week he was late twice, so that was £20, of course he only got paid £40 ... the structure of his brain was such that he said, "It's not my fault," and I said, "Well, whose is it?" and he said, "Well, I go to sleep and I don't wake up" ... I spent a lot of time with him, I tell you. We used to ring up and there would be no answer, his parents would be at work, he'd oversleep. Every time he didn't turn up I'd send someone round his house, and nine times out of ten he'd knock on the door and there'd be no answer, so in the end we shouted "Police!" through the letterbox and that got him up.'

Petchey identified in the youngster an innocence and lack of understanding about life which Arsenal had responded to by rejecting him, a decision which still baffles him. He was convinced a bright future lay ahead for his new signing and predicted great things.

'He was influenced by everything. I said to him one time, "All that glitters is not gold, sometimes it's a reflection." If anyone calls you a name forget it, go out and play, just laugh and walk away. If you do that, after a time it will be "Hello, Laurie". That's how it will turn out, everybody will want to know you. You keep playing like you are, you'll be picked for England under-21s, you'll catch fire. Everybody will want to know you, it's going to be a great life.'

Football promised a great life with great hours too. Training began at 10 a.m. and would be over by 12.30, leaving the rest of the day free. As soon as Cunningham and Fisher became friends they began to explore London together. Neither of them fitted the mould of the stereotypical footballer who relaxed with a few pints after training in the nearest pub or played a round of golf at the local course. Fisher says that they simply did not want to be around boozing footballers all the time. 'We used to hate those big dimpled pint mugs, we wanted a glass of wine, there was a lovely feel about it. No footballer would ever drink wine, it was pints of lager and lime.' The pair would talk about music, cinema and fashion, get the tube into the West End to see a film or just look around, soaking up the atmosphere. Elegant wine bars were to be found on Oxford Street and Baker Street, and, most glamorous of all, Morton's Piano Bar on Berkeley Square in Mayfair, where Cunningham would blow his weekly wages on bottles of champagne with the new friends he made there. The sheer excitement of setting foot in this rarefied, exclusive world where nobody knew you were a footballer unless you told them so, thrilled the would-be sophisticates. They would got to the King's Road, Chelsea where Cunningham would jot down notes and sketch ideas for outfits into his drawing pad.

Quite how distinctive the pair had become was brought home to Fisher when they played for Orient reserves away against Southend United. Arriving on the team bus, Cunningham and Fisher were sitting with their good friend and teammate Tony Grealish, a loud and voluble second-generation Irish immigrant who had been brought up in a pub in Paddington. As the bus pulled in to the Southend ground they noticed their opponents soberly dressed in club suits, ties and dark shoes, the uniform of the young footballer. Bobby Fisher recalls the moment the Orient players disembarked: 'There was Tony Grealish, big beard, loon pants, platform shoes and a jacket. I came off with a sparkly jacket, silk trousers and high platform boots and a big Afro. You could see the Southend boys going, "What's this? The circus has arrived." And then Laurie came off with a gangster suit, shirt and tie, tiepin, two-tone shoes, fedora and a cane, and it was like "Oh, man! What's happening here?" ... You look back at it now and it was quite exceptional, you looked at it then and it was just part of him.'

Cunningham was absorbing influences in the way he dressed from numerous sources. The radical designs he saw in a select few shops in places like the King's Road encouraged him to experiment and mix and match second-hand clothing with new, small-run designer items. He was beginning to personalise his look by scouring markets in Camden Passage in Islington, where good-quality, well-made forties and fifties clothing – jackets, shoes and ties – were sold in bundles on the pavement. Styling original 1940s clothing into his wardrobe created an entirely individual, curated look, assembled with fastidious attention to detail; clothes that ordinarily may not have gone together did when worn by him as a complete outfit. He made them look good. His enviable dress sense instantly singled him out as different and attracted plenty of attention. Fisher remembers, 'He had to be different, whatever. Laurie's biggest fear was becoming like everyone else, becoming the norm, he really didn't want to.' Not many people looked like Cunningham at the time and it took some front to dress in such a way, particularly in the world of professional football where the sarcastic comments from teammates must have come thick and fast. At first glance someone dressed so lavishly might be assumed to be an extrovert demanding centre stage, but this was not the case. An introverted – at times awkward – teenager who was cautious with strangers, the clothes he loved to wear sent out a message so powerful that they succeeded in deflecting attention away from the person wearing them. His individuality could be communicated non-verbally, thus avoiding difficult questions, and if people wanted to believe he was up front and flash then so be it; they didn't know the real person after all. This self-invention, or creation of a persona, spoke of a desire to not conform – a feeling common to many teenagers and by no means unique to Cunningham – which he chose to express in a strikingly imaginative way. By dressing in such a distinctive manner he was saying that football was not the only thing that mattered, it did not define him, and clothes could be used as a tool to explore different aspects of his personality.

As Petchey noted he was 'influenced by everything', which may sound like criticism of his naivety, but can also be read as a receptiveness to new ideas and a willingness to engage in the world beyond football. If outside interests clashed with training Petchey was often left in the lurch and, as we have seen, compelled to fine his player for it. Fisher refers to the moods that sometimes overtook Cunningham where he seemed to be present more in body than in spirit: 'If he focused in on something that was it, games and everything else would go out of the window. They wouldn't be important, something else would come up that focused his attention.' This focus was integral to the nature of his talent and what may have been considered eccentric or odd behaviour is indicative of how his mind worked. Petchey instinctively understood this, recognising in Cunningham a maverick streak that was as brilliant as it was exasperating. At times he wondered if he could ever win his complex young player over: 'The old eyes flashed when I fined him, but for all that I loved the spark that made him,' he says.

Cunningham made his professional debut on 3 August 1974 against West Ham in the Texaco Cup, a short-lived tournament involving teams from the UK and Ireland, and made his full League debut two months later against Oldham Athletic at Brisbane Road. Then, in December, he was picked for an away match against Millwall – a club notorious for the vehemence and violence of its supporters – along with the club's two other black players, Bobby Fisher and Ricky Heppolette. Millwall's fearsome reputation was enough to deter even the Orient fans from travelling in any great number and when the trio took to the field they were almost certainly the only blacks inside the ground. The players' tunnel was situated, intimidatingly, directly behind one of the goals and flanked by hostile home fans penned in behind a wire cage. As Orient emerged they were greeted with jeers; the black players were spat at and met with a chorus of racist chants and obscenities. Bananas were hurled onto the pitch and a carving knife was reportedly later found by the side of the pitch. Petchey had earlier warned his players not to play too near the touchline if they could help it, in case fans threw ball bearings at them. Fisher remembers the pressure he felt every time he got the ball and the tangible sense of hatred he and his fellow black players provoked by their mere presence in this tight and highly charged atmosphere. The match finished 1–1, with Cunningham scoring a late equaliser, and at the final whistle the players began their thankless walk back to the tunnel in front of the snarling Millwall faithful. As Cunningham and Fisher approached the touchline the fans' hatred reached a new level.

Fisher takes up the story. 'So we were on the pitch and perhaps felt a little bit safe. We put our arms around each other and blew them a kiss and then gave them the Black Power salute ... the tension changed from hatred to "now we want to kill you and we will lynch you". They jumped up onto the fence and four or five coppers dragged us down the tunnel and threw us into the changing room. A copper came in and said whatever happens do not leave this room and closed the door behind us. An inspector came in about two minutes later and said, "Do you know you have incited a riot. We could charge you." We thought: have you been here for the last ninety minutes?'

After being held back in the dressing room for an hour the Orient team were finally allowed to board the team coach under police protection, with the warning that if any stones were thrown to lie flat on the floor, as motorcycle outriders quickly escorted them back across London. The irony of the police inspector attempting to blame Cunningham and Fisher for provoking a riot was indicative of the way racism in football was perceived at the time. Fisher insists the Black Power salute was a spontaneous response to the barracking he, Cunningham and Heppolette had received throughout the game. He says it was not pre-planned and that neither of them fully understood the political significance of the gesture; it was just something they had seen American black athletes do in the 1968 Olympics. It looked good and in the heat of the moment they wanted to emulate them. But they were both aware of the significance of making such a salute at The Den, the home of Millwall Football Club. The club that celebrates its self-styled nastiness with the chant 'no one likes us, we don't care', was a bastion of racism in 1974. To make such a gesture, in the 'Lion's Den', meant more than it would at any other ground in the country. As Fisher comments, the implication to the Millwall fans that night was clear: 'This is your greatest fear, this is really going to kill you, and you can't do a thing about it.' There were no headlines in the press the following day; the issue of racist abuse inside football grounds was seen as something that was not a problem for clubs, rather it was a symptom of the wider ills of society. Nobody was ever thrown out of a ground for racial abuse or for threatening conduct. If the subject was ever mentioned at all in boardrooms it was probably met with palms up, outstretched hands and a shrug of the shoulders.

As Cunningham was selected for the first team more regularly, Petchey asked key players Heppolette and Grealish to keep an eye out for any signs that the physical and verbal abuse he was getting might start to affect his performance. In a Cup game against Derby County in 1975 he was brought on as a substitute and started to destroy the left back, with his pace and agility. During the game a couple of Derby players gave him some verbal abuse with one reportedly saying, 'Here's the banana between my feet, monkey: come and get it.' No doubt this was just seen as gamesmanship and all part of the game by a pair of experienced pros trying to gain a psychological advantage over a tricky young opponent, but Petchey was irritated enough by it to single out that game as a spiteful example of the sustained abuse Cunningham received. Yet he also approved of his reaction to the kicks and barbs: 'The left back gave him an unmerciful kicking, people were throwing bananas on the pitch. At half-time he asked me, "What do I do about the bananas?" I said collect them up and give them to the linesman. Don't worry about it. He didn't but he saw the funny side.' He adds that he generally advised him to '"Walk away, don't ever show them that you have been hurt, or that you resent it, just walk away." And to his credit he did that. I never saw him retaliate or do something to show that he'd been hurt. He'd often come off the pitch and he'd be very quiet and it was then that one of the players would sort him out. "Paddy" Grealish looked after him a lot; he was buoyant, you couldn't subdue "Paddy", he was good, especially with Laurie.'

By early 1975 Orient were gaining a reputation as an improving footballing side and Cunningham was given an extended run in the first team for the last quarter of the season. He was great to watch and caught the eye with his distinctive, upright and on-his-toes running style, looking like a black Nureyev gliding across the Brisbane Road mudbath *en-pointe* as if it were the stage of the Royal Ballet. The ballet comparison is not inappropriate. Cunningham appreciated the strength and agility of professional dancers, in particular ballet dancers, whom he admired for their poise and control – and astonishingly was offered a place on tour with the US ensemble The Dance Theatre of Harlem when its founder Arthur Mitchell wrote to the club stating his admiration for the player. In a letter he described Cunningham as 'the best athletic mover I have seen in ten to fifteen years teaching dance ... incredible control of movement, with the ability to stop quickly and turn quickly.' It was an offer Cunningham gave serious thought to, even asking the baffled Petchey if he should say yes to it: who had to remind him it was he who paid his wages each week.

In an attempt to change his players' mental attitude Petchey introduced stretching exercises based on ballet warm-ups to his training sessions and brought in a trampolinist to demonstrate core muscle fitness and agility. Innovations like these must have struck a chord with Cunningham's open-minded, alternative view of life. He took an interest in yoga and started taking karate lessons with his best friend Bert. Martial arts were popular at the time and crossing over into mainstream popular culture and the films of Bruce Lee and Jackie Chan were favourites with Cunningham and Fisher on their trips to the West End. The maturing teenager was starting to think about the mental side of his game more too and beginning to realise that if his head was clear and focused it would help improve his performance on the pitch. In what is now known in sporting parlance as 'being in the zone', he told a reporter in January 1976, 'I've only scored four goals this season and I need to sharpen up my game in front of goal. I've hardened my mental approach since taking up yoga. Before a game I sit quietly in the corner of the dressing room and think about what I must do out on the pitch. The silent spell helps my concentration.'

Getting his players to slow down and think about the game in this way proved an uphill task for Petchey who struggled to get the philosophy of push and run over to his squad. Basic football training can very quickly become dull. In an effort to freshen things up and to stop his players simply kicking the ball as far and as hard as they could, Petchey introduced basketball into daily training. His hope was the players would think quickly on their feet, release the ball and move into space for a return pass. The reality proved to be less beneficial as players soon began to run with the ball and play rugby with it instead. He admitted ruefully, 'If you couldn't get it with their hands you weren't going to get it with their feet.' Cunningham's natural athleticism stood out and he excelled at everything from cross-country runs and sprints to smaller, more spontaneous pieces of skill that marked him out as special. Fisher recalls a simple move that summed up Cunningham's off-the-cuff unconventional mind. During training one day the ball landed on the top of the net above the goal. Usually somebody would jump up and punch the ball back out and on to the ground and the game would continue, but on this occasion Cunningham walked casually up to the goal. 'It was a real throwaway thing. He just came up and did a scissors kick and flipped it out and as it came out he caught the ball with his foot, controlled it, and rolled it back out to a teammate.' Superb natural fitness, evident since childhood, impressed his manager: 'Laurie was a great athlete. He could run like a deer and that was his greatest strength. We did cross-country at a police training centre near Croydon, and it was hard, it had 150 steps on the course. Laurie would do it and not break sweat.'

As the 1976 season progressed Cunningham's name was starting to attract praise in the local press. In a match against Fulham at Craven Cottage he gave World Cup legend and former England captain Bobby Moore a torrid afternoon, which he rounded off by scoring the winning goal. His electrifying pace and terrific stamina frightened most defenders, who, in struggling to keep up, attempted to stop him with crushing high tackles. In order to survive he relied on his extraordinary balance to ride challenges without breaking stride in a flowing continuous move resembling a tap dancer's barrel roll. The ability to outfox antagonistic players with such elan gracefully highlighted the gulf between him and his more flat-footed opponents. In the book *Leyton Orient Greats* by Matt Simpson, Orient fan Tom Collins remembered the pride home fans felt watching him play: 'We knew that we had something special and could never understand the hate and vilification towards black people. There was this very proud thing about Laurie being at the Orient. Laurie had attitude and ability in a team full of triers and workhorses. It was almost as if he was imposing a reverse superiority, telling all around him that black people were superior to their white players.'

The dressing-room meditation before games began to pay off as Cunningham started scoring goals more regularly, increasing his strike rate to eight goals for the season from thirty-five starts, not perhaps the most impressive tally, but enough to make him top scorer for the club that season. Again in *Leyton Orient Greats*, the *Walthamstow Guardian* report on one goal scored against Hull City reads: 'Laurie Cunningham's excellence lifted him above the other players and left Hull City gasping. He scored a marvellous goal and conjured up several more chances. The home side were anxiously searching for a breakthrough when Cunningham pulled out one of his many tricks in the thirty-fourth minute. He took the ball, controlled it on the edge of the box, looked up and chipped it precisely into the far corner over the keeper's head. It was a goal that would have graced any ground in the country.'

The improvement in Cunningham's concentration levels was encouraging for his manager but his idiosyncrasies remained. There were days when his focus was elsewhere and in one instance he vanished for an entire week. Missing a day's training in Cunningham's case was not wholly unexpected but when he did not turn up the next day, an angry Petchey asked Fisher to go and find him. Repeated telephone calls to the Cunningham home went unanswered and as Saturday came there was still no sign of the missing player. Puzzlement turned to concern: missing a game, especially a home game, without good reason was just not done. Kick-off came and went and to add insult to injury Orient were beaten. The mood at the team meeting the following Monday morning was downbeat. Ten minutes after it had begun footsteps were heard moving softly along the tiled corridor outside. Fisher recognised his friend's unhurried, gliding walk. After a few choice words Petchey asked Cunningham where he had been all week. The surprising reply came back that he had been at home and did not have the bus fare to get in and there was nobody else to borrow it from. When pressed as to why, if he had been at home all week, he hadn't answered the telephone, he replied because it was downstairs and he was upstairs. Fisher puts this down to 'a little bit of insanity' on Cunningham's part; it is certainly eccentric behaviour and Petchey seems to have accepted it as part and parcel of who Cunningham was, reflecting more than once, 'He was some character, I can tell you'. Maybe it was some form of mild behavioural disorder which in those days might be put down to moodiness or arrogance.

The football writer Brain Glanville, who had a fondness for Orient and admired what Petchey was trying to achieve at the club, wrote a cover piece for the *Sunday Times Magazine* in March 1976 asking, 'Will Laurie Cunningham be the first coloured footballer to play for England?' In it he identifies what he considers his subject's character flaw: 'Cunningham for all his courtesy and enthusiasm will periodically vanish to the bewilderment of his family as much as the club, however often they fine him for it.' The article puts Cunningham in the context of the black footballers who had gone before him in the English game and relishes the prospect of him and similar players breaking through into the full national side, asking, 'If Laurie Cunningham could only play for England who knows what energies might be unleashed?' Infuriatingly for Glanville, who must have sympathised with Petchey, the arranged interview with Cunningham never took place because he vanished again; instead Glanville spent two hours drinking tea with his mother Mavis at the family home in Tottenham. To his credit he still profiled the player with equanimity.

It was rare for a footballer to grace the cover of the *Sunday Times Magazine*, let alone a black one from a lowly Second Division club. Cunningham's profile was dramatically raised by the coverage and his name began to spread beyond the world of football. His photograph began to appear in more and more magazines and on television. Like George Best before him he was starting to become a pop culture personality who represented something more than just football.

4

YOUNG HEARTS RUN FREE

Laurie Cunningham liked to sketch and paint, could play the piano and appreciated architecture. In the conservative world of English football he was something of a Renaissance man. He was fastidious about clothes and took great care over his appearance. He understood the tactile quality of cloth and how it affected the cut and drape of a garment. Silk was his favourite material. Ever since his school days he had dressed in a distinctive and precise way – even within the limitations of school uniform he made amendments and additions to make himself stand out. His friend Robert Johnson recalls the impression he made: 'Anything in fashion Laurie would have it before anybody regardless of race, colour, creed; by the time he was fifteen years old you could see the change in him, see he loved to dress up. Whenever you went somewhere you never knew what Laurence was going to come as.'

Cunningham's interest in clothes placed him at the centre of a London fashion elite that sprang from the streets and dance halls of inner-London. Its members, a small group of working-class taste-makers, created an original yet retro look in the dive bars, pub back rooms and sweat boxes of London's fledgling nightclub scene. The black soul boys are briskly skimmed over in the history of British youth culture yet they were at the vanguard of fashion and music in the mid-1970s. Almost too few in number to be called a scene and too fugitive to be pinned down, their heritage is witnessed in the club culture of today and the continued appeal of such menswear staples as vintage, country-casual and utility wear. Cunningham was a rare phenomenon who traversed the worlds of professional football, street fashion and underground music and was a key member of a group of sophisticated black youths who created an original identity through their love of music, dance and fashion.

One of the best dancers on the scene, Leon Herbert, who was born in 1955, exemplified their proud attitude and like Cunningham was obsessed with clothes from an early age. He explains, 'I started buying my own clothes aged eleven. I got Levi's from a shop at Angel which was the only shop that sold them. My first suit was Tonik, it was tailor made, and I wore it with cordovan brogues; they were made of a special soft leather that didn't crack on the break. Back then highly polished shoes were the thing, black, brown and cherry, they were the colours you saw more than anything else. There was a walk that went with the clothes too, it was all one thing you see, like a peacock. I didn't realise I just did it. So I wore a suit, tie pin and hanky, it was flashy, flashy, flashy. It was a dressing-up competition, the polished shoe – you didn't want to step on someone's shoes, they would cut you up. It was the Ivy League James Brown look, gleaming Tonik suits and brogues. I remember going to a party called Sir Coxsone and I walked to the door and I thought I was on a catwalk! The girls, the guys, everyone was dressed up to the point where it didn't make sense! I thought I was cool but I wasn't, they were beyond me. Some of the colours of the shirts! When you have a Tonik suit on at night and the light catches it, the shine! It gleams man, it gleams! And the shoes and socks! I'm a kid, all I had was this one suit, but I'm feasting on all this information.'

The five years he spent at Leyton Orient between 1972 and 1977 gave Cunningham the opportunity to fully explore London. Travelling to the King's Road in Chelsea with his well-honed eye for detail he would have been exposed to sights and places a world away from his home in Finsbury Park. Glamour was in short supply in this period and the King's Road, which still traded on its former glory as the centre of swinging London, remained an outpost of colour and hedonism. It was where the hip London crowd hung out in a creative and idiosyncratic environment. To a black teenager with a love of clothes it suggested a radically different way of life to that of the professional footballer. Yet Cunningham would also have been an outsider here too. Black faces on the King's Road were few and far between and seen as exotic. The film-maker Don Letts, who ran the clothing shop Acme Attractions there, says, 'I started working on the King's Road at sixteen. I learnt more working there than I ever learnt at school. I was wearing kohl eyeliner and a clutch bag and buying *L'Uomo Vogue*. There wasn't more than ten black guys working on the King's Road – we all knew each other – all the time I was working there from 1972 to 1978.' Cunningham and his friend Bert Jordine loved being part of the fashion parade where everyone was dressed to the nines and there was always something happening. Avant-garde shops and secondhand stalls offered rich pickings for someone with a good eye. At the forefront of cutting-edge style was the radical punk boutique Sex, owned by Malcolm

McLaren and Vivienne Westwood. Jordine recalls visiting with Cunningham, 'We used to go to Sex for the tops as they did things that were different – it was cut differently – he liked to show off his physique.'

Cunningham would have been familiar with the 'Windrush' look that his father's generation wore, well-cut suits worn with hats and polished shoes. Most memorable of all was the 'zoot' suit – the outlandish and highly stylised suit, with a long drape jacket and exaggerated baggy trousers that suggested the pride and self-sufficiency of its wearer.

The suit carried an outsider reputation, since the 1930s it had been worn by blacks and hispanics in America and quickly became affiliated with the Jazz scene in the major industrial cities. In 1975 Cunningham was earning enough to have suits made that explicitly referenced the 'zoot' suit. One morning on his way to training he chanced upon a find which became the catalyst for a style that came to define the London soul boy. 'The Great Gatsby' look as it became known was the first vintage youth look and was named after the 1974 Robert Redford film. Although the book and film are set in 1920s Jazz Age America, the pastel coloured suits in the film have a later, more contemporary feel that along with the 'zoot' suits of the 1940s inspired a smart soul boy look that became known simply as the 'Gatsby' look. Soho tailor Mark Powell, an original east London soul boy from the time, puts the style into context when he says, 'The 1970s corrupted fashion so badly even Morecambe & Wise were wearing flares! The earlier mod scene was contemporary, all about contemporary cut and styling. The Gatsby look was fashionable as it made you look more individual to be going back to the 1940s and 1950s for your style influences; there were only a certain number of people that were like that at the time. To be that into it was unique. The only people who would speak to you were people on the same tip as you, but that was part of the buzz, getting remarks and comments walking along the street.'

Cunningham's timely discovery took place outside a shop that was undergoing renovation on Leyton High Street. In a clear-out the shopkeeper had left a pair of large travel trunks outside on the pavement. On closer inspection he discovered that the trunks were full of original wartime clothing wrapped in cellophane. As he rummaged through the packages he realised what he had found – shirts, a pair of shoes, a hat and pinstripe suit – all in immaculate condition and hardly worn. The shopkeeper sold him the lot for a few pounds. He loved the authenticity of the treasure trove; the feel and weight of the suit, the elegant chocolate brown and tan co-respondent shoes, and the dramatic high-crowned antelope fedora with dark contrasting band. With one stroke of luck he had found a fully formed look. The only drawback was the colour of the suit: he had disliked navy since his days in school uniform, but that was a minor hitch and easily fixed. What really mattered most was the original cut and lines of the suit that gave him a template to work from. He found a veteran Jewish tailor in Stratford, conveniently close to the Brisbane Road ground, and ordered a copy of the suit to be made up from his sketches.

Cunningham's interpretation of the Gatsby look is both interesting and subtle. The styling may not be entirely accurate but the outfit is assembled with a connoisseur's sensitivity. It is a prime example of what makes the soul boy culture at this time so distinctive. The finished look has been coordinated from multiple sources to produce a unique result. His insistence on details such as original weight wool, original hat and shoes paired with silk shirt and tie put him in the tradition of the English dandy. The whole look has a street quality as well; it is not too polished or coordinated, but uses the forties' suit as an outline and enhances it with modern styling. A photograph taken on the muddy pitch at Brisbane Road reveals a young man showing the world he is more than a footballer. The nonchalant stance belongs to someone who understands the importance of clothes.

The Gatsby look was the starting point for a style kept fresh by constant reinvention. By putting together borrowed clothes and secondhand items with famous names from English tailoring, a nuanced look could be created. Cunningham's contemporary on the dance floor Dez Parkes remembers: 'Some of us would take our father's 'zoot' suits because that was cut in the perfect way, the bagginess to show off certain moves when you were dancing. We were into the forties' look so we would buy Harris tweeds, Prince of Wales check stuff. There was a top tailor in Carnaby Street and a material shop in Wardour Street where you could buy your cloth, get your high-waisted pants made. It was a nice style. We would wear fur coats, satchel bags and scarves – it was very American, very Hollywood. I used to wear hacking jackets with a cricket jumper tied round my shoulders or cream trousers with a black or red belt to accentuate the waistline, which was important. We would save up or hustle to buy shirts from Turnbull & Asser, go to Aquascutum or Lillywhites. We would go into the club looking slick.'

Steve Salvari, from Wood Green in north London, who danced alongside Cunningham as a teenager loved the theatricality of the Gatsby look and laughs at the lengths he used to go to to get the right clothes: 'We discovered a shop in Petticoat Lane and it would be pandemonium. They sold these proper original thirties and forties shoes. It was a real beaten-up old shop and on a Saturday it was so packed you couldn't get in there. It was never organised properly. You would see a pair of shoes in the window and say "I want them" and have to check through loads of boxes to get them. Honestly it was pandemonium. For hats there was Agnello & Davide, they did proper gangster hats and two-tone dancing shoes. They had a shop on Charing Cross Road and a theatrical suppliers on Tottenham Court Road.' He cites the example of a friend of his who was so particular that he refused to sit down on the tube in case it creased his trousers. The careful owner of half a dozen pairs of white trousers, he carried a piece of brown paper in his pocket whenever he went out to put down on chairs before sitting on them.

The Gatsby look was also a reaction to hard times. By 1974 years of poor labour relations and economic paralysis left the country in political stalemate. The Conservative government led by Edward Heath suffered a series of bruising encounters with the unions and in a drastic attempt to counter the striking miners introduced the 'three-day week' directive. This was an emergency measure which restricted the commercial supply of electricity to businesses and rationed it to three consecutive days a week. For small businesses, it was a disaster. Lloyd Johnson, a fashion retailer, whose stall Johnson & Johnson in Kensington Market was an important supplier to the soul boys, was forced to improvise to keep his business afloat. Unable to place orders with textile manufacturers who gave priority to their larger customers he began to style second-hand clothes in such a way as to make them look ultra-modern. He talks in fascinating detail about the clothes he sold to the soul boys, and in particular the demob suit. 'I found a place in Leman Street in Aldgate. There was a chicken slaughterhouse in the area so the whole atmosphere was full of that, you came out covered in chicken down and feathers, dust and muck. They had a deal with military quartermasters and they were buying up brown paper parcels that were stamped s/b or d/b (single-breasted or double-breasted) and they were all demob suits. You couldn't open them up to look at them, you had to buy the parcels intact. So I'd buy fifty of them and nearly all of them were great. We sold tons of that. Suits were a reaction to the scruffiness of men's fashion which had gone downhill rapidly after 1973. An American came to my stall one day and invited me over to a bonded warehouse in Borough. He was the son of a US rag yard merchant who had shipped a container of stuff to London, full of forties and fifties US clothes. I thought I can't let this guy go down the King's Road. We got the best pick of everything. He was bringing over salt and pepper fleck 'zoot' jackets, 1940s stuff, things like classic flap and patch gaberdine shirts from the forties. I was buying things for peanuts that now go for hundreds of pounds. We made four-piece suits with a newsboy cap where everything matched in light colours, pastel pink and blues. I sold loads of white v-neck Airtex tops from the army. We used to dye them yellow, pink and blue; they looked great with pegs and any form of mad sunglasses. In the early seventies nobody wanted pleats in their trousers, it was all about narrow hips. I started doing Oxford bags with short jackets, we called them Charlie Chaplin suits. To get them out cheap we made them out of white cotton poplin and we'd dye them different colours, put them with a Hawaiian shirt; it looked like 1930s cruise wear.'

Nikki Hare-Brown was a girl who loved to dance. Born in 1960 she grew up in north London and attended Parliament Hill Girls' School near to where her family lived in well-to-do Hampstead. As a teenager she appeared in photo shoots for fashion magazines and later modelled clothes for hip local label Swanky Modes in Camden. Her open-minded parents, both involved in show business indulged their daughter's talent for dancing and taught her basic steps in the family living room. She recalls, 'We used to jazz jive. My parents coached me through because they used to do it at the Lyceum when they first met.' Funk music arrived in the UK in 1975 at just the right time for her youthful exuberance. 'I had to go out and dance just to get rid of this energy,' she says. Sunday night, when funk was played, was the best night for dancing at the Tottenham Royal. The ballroom – owned and run by the Mecca company on Tottenham High Road – was a site of pilgrimage for hundreds of devoted followers who answered its call to dance each week. With a revolving stage, large expanse of sprung flooring and potted palms dotted here and there, the club possessed the dubious glamour of the time. Since the War the venue had been a popular meeting place for teenagers from all across north London. Legions of mods had descended on their scooters in the 1960s for the packed-out soul all-nighters held there.

She remembers the atmosphere there as glamorous and full of promise. Nikki first noticed Cunningham there when he began dancing next to her one Sunday. Apart from admiring his dancing she remembers the clothes he was wearing that night. Reflecting the more casual soul boy look, it being Sunday night, Cunningham was dressed in baggy workwear 'carpenter'-style jeans, polished flat-soled shoes and a short-sleeved American gas attendant's shirt, untucked and billowing as he moved around. The retro blue shirt, with contrasting coloured pleats on the back, had the name 'Paul' embroidered above the breast pocket, and she assumed that was his name, although the pair did not speak. Approving of his dress sense but not much else – 'he looked a bit spotty' – she continued to dance with her friends for the rest of the evening. Cunningham was there again the following week dancing nearby, and the week after, when he finally broke the ice and spoke to her. Still under the impression his name was 'Paul' (it was actually his middle name and frequently used by members of his family), when she saw him on television a few days later coming on as a substitute for Leyton Orient captioned as 'Laurie Cunningham' she felt cheated, so much so, that when he rang her later that evening to ask her out she refused to speak to him and told him not to bother calling again. Such an emotional response obviously appealed to Cunningham, as undeterred, he sat outside her house until she relented and gave him a second chance. Speaking in a newspaper article a few years later about their relationship he talked of their first date, 'Nikki kept me waiting for half an hour at Finsbury Park tube station. No girl had ever kept me waiting before. I was angry at first, then very intrigued, I'd met my match.'

Cunningham had always been popular with girls and one female friend recalls his effortless style. She even remembers that his football shorts at school seemed to be more fitted than anyone else's. Whatever he wore he looked good she says. Robert Johnson says that his friend had an unaffected charisma which girls loved. At school being the best at football is enough to elevate a person to special status, but in the case of Cunningham he seemed to be a natural at so many things, from art to athletics, that counted with teenagers. Johnson says of his friend that 'he was quiet spoken but great with the girls, he could handle the girls better than I did' – and whilst he had a strict Jamaican mother he remembers Cunningham's parents as among the more relaxed of the time. At Leyton Orient Cunningham was a hit with George Petchey's daughter at the club Christmas party one year. 'She was quite taken with him because of the way he was dancing in his white trousers,' remembers his wife Moll, to which George adds sardonically, 'He would wear flares if it killed him!' The sex appeal and charm he possessed as a young man went over well with women, yet his modest nature also kept him popular among male friends who could easily have resented him because of it.

Around the age of sixteen when couples from school were starting to pair up, Johnson noticed that his friend tended to prefer white girls. He told him he felt they were easier to deal with and usually had far less attitude than most of the black girls they knew. It is interesting that he was attracted to Nikki who as a strong-minded fifteen-year-old sounds as if she had plenty of attitude of her own. Perhaps he was looking for a more substantial relationship as he approached his twenties and apart from the obvious physical attraction the couple felt towards each other there was a quick bond that neither had experienced before. The seven years that they were together were the most significant in Cunningham's footballing life. He met Nikki on the dance floor when he was starting out in the game, she was with him when he signed for West Bromwich Albion for over £100,000 and she was with him when he moved to Spain in an unprecedented £1 million deal joining Real Madrid in 1979. For such a young couple they shared a deep understanding of each other's temperament. With Nikki he had found someone who loved the things he loved as much as he did.

She was also the passport to a different lifestyle. His desire to explore interests outside of football with a girlfriend who was just as enthusiastic and adventurous as he was led to him spending less and less time with teammates as the couple discovered the broad exciting world of London in the 1970s. Her father, Mike, an entertainer and comedian got on well with Cunningham's mother – they shared similar friendly outgoing personalities – while Cunningham's father's love of music fitted her parents liking for big-band jazz. Nikki remembers her parents parties as open-door affairs where a wide variety of people were invited. Friends and associates from the worlds of music, entertainment and sport rubbed shoulders with neighbours and her teenage friends, and the festivities went on long into the night. Keith Cunningham recalls watching his brother with Nikki on the dance floor: 'Nobody could dance like my brother and especially him and Nikki they were like a team, a duo, she could coordinate with him every move he made; she was always there with him, she never made a mistake. To watch them two dancing ... it's a bad thing they never had camera phones in them times. Everybody used to stand and watch them.' For a couple who loved to dance London was full of interesting venues, from Maunkberry's on Jermyn Street where the funk music was hard and heavy and played until 6.00 a.m. to the underground fashion haunt Global Village, an important early punk venue on the Strand where soul boys and dyed-haired punks rubbed shoulders with each other, to the Purple Pussycat in Finchley, a gay club that played great music – the choices were many and could include a session at Ronnie Scott's on Thursday, Crackers on Friday lunchtime followed by the 100 club on Oxford Street on Saturday night and the Tottenham Royal on Sunday.

The Thames television children's programme *Magpie* profiled Cunningham with surprising depth in 1976. In the programme he comes across as polite and unassuming in footage that shows him training at the five-a-side pitch at Leyton Orient, cooking for his mother at home and decorating his bedroom, as well as dancing – albeit rather self-consciously, for the camera, in the Bird's Nest in Muswell Hill with Nikki. He is asked by the interviewer if black youths face any particular problems in the game and replies with a wry smile and an eye-roll that 'Yeah, it's more difficult because the attitude managers have is that black kids are dainty on the ball and tend not to be physical, you know. When there is a ball to be won I'll be there, and usually get a kick afterwards ... They (managers) think I'm a chicken if I jump out of the way afterwards, but if you are going for a ball and you know you are going to win it in a certain way, and tap it to one side of the man, then you have avoided being kicked, and also you've got the ball at the same time, but managers tend to think that is a bit girlish, and dainty, to jump out of the way.'

Looking great in black polo neck jumper and dark flared trousers he is filmed cooking his 'speciality' lamb and rice for his mother, Mavis, before donning overalls and painting his bedroom wall which he says he finds relaxing and does 'as much as I can before I get bored' – before moving on to show his Volvo sports coupé with its 'champagne fur' lining the seats, roof and interior door panels. The segment where he is shown dancing with Nikki is obviously set up for the camera, but even so the pair display an easy grace and the film is overlaid with a voice-over from Cunningham describing how he has learnt 'Afro-Rock' dance – which he describes as a mixture of ballet and funk that improves his coordination and can 'get you out of trouble quickly' in a game. Shot just before his career took off, he is realistic about his shortcomings saying he hopes to play for England in the World Cup one day, but needs to keep focused: 'I can be really good one day and the next day be a bit dodgy and not play too well, but I'm trying my best to develop it and keep a ninety minute game every Saturday.'

Today Nikki lives in a small coastal town in Cornwall where she works as a wedding planner and rents out family properties as holiday lets. I meet her in the bar of a small comfortable hotel. Her hair is long, but lighter and flecked with grey now, and her eye for detail becomes apparent when I ask her to talk about her teenage years in London. When I show her old photographs of Cunningham in his soul boy pomp, she quickly becomes animated and recalls with obvious enjoyment the songs, clubs and fashions of the time. An assured, direct person, which she partly attributes to having to grow up quickly when she moved to Madrid as a nineteen-year-old, she speaks freely about her years together with Cunningham. Reflecting on their first meeting at the Tottenham Royal, she says she looked older than her fifteen years and her confident manner may have meant she came across as worldly-wise but beneath it all she was just a naive teenager. She did not find Cunningham attractive straightaway yet soon fell for his unassuming way; she says, 'I didn't fancy him at first but later there was something about him that you couldn't help but love, my parents felt it too. He was lost in this world. For the first couple of years we became best friends really, you know walking me home with a kiss. That's as innocent as it was,' adding, 'the dancing came out of it, from the innocence and a love of it,' but it was not something he promoted. If he was a trendsetter in fashion terms whom some people looked to for ideas, he was not conscious of it. 'The clothes that he wore would be copied a week or two later by others, you could see that as a woman, but he wouldn't be aware of it. As elaborate as he was in his dress and dance he was a very shy man outside of family and friends. He was never arrogant.'

When they got together they spent most of the time sharing their ideas about life and a casual friendship developed between the two families. The Cunningham house in Lancaster Road, a large three-storey place, became a second home for Nikki and she spent many hours there and got to know the family well. If he wasn't working, Elias, who sometimes wore a hair net indoors to keep his hair clean, would be listening to ska or jazz on the record player, and periodically quoted Martin Luther King – whose portrait hung on the living-room wall – to his boys. If the couple decided on impulse to take off for a few days without telling anybody an exasperated Mavis would worry, 'Where in the world are they now? My heart will give out!'

The pair would climb onto the rooftop of Lancaster Road to stare at the stars and jump across to the neighbouring roof. She laughs at the memory of them climbing a ladder to the top storey to sneak into Keith's bedroom, where his precious record collection was kept under lock and key. Cunningham placed matchsticks underneath the window frame beforehand so it could be opened from the outside. The innocence extended to reading fairy tales aloud to each other and marvelling at the natural world. Nikki says, 'We used to wonder, we used to look at trees, at 200-year-old oaks and think about the history of them, we used to go to museums, really plain stuff that people would never imagine that he enjoyed – but within that we had to go out dancing to get our fix. If we weren't out dancing we were at home dancing.' His favourite film was Disney's *The Jungle Book*, which Nikki claims they watched nine times together. It is easy to see why it appealed to him with its beautiful colours and memorable song and dance routines that referenced the Harlem jazz dancers they so admired. On Sunday mornings they would sleep in late and watch television. When the lunchtime football highlights show *The Big Match* came on Cunningham would not necessarily be interested in watching it, especially if it clashed with a Hollywood musical on the other side. His favourite star was Fred Astaire; he loved his flair and the way he danced with a partner, and the young pair tirelessly practised the moves from his films. They also perfected Donald O'Connor's famous running backflip from the film *Singin' in the Rain* – it was just a case of mind over matter. Cunningham had finished with football for the week and didn't need to be part of that world any more, he wanted to get on with the rest of life. Nikki states, 'Dancers inspired him, not footballers.'

They shared a love of clothes and tried out different looks on each other. 'We'd go to theatrical costumiers off Charlotte Street; they would sell stuff off, straight out of the door, or sometimes if they were closing down you could pick up stuff. My dad had friends at Pinewood Studios so we could get access there. My dad had a lot of names and addresses, so if we wanted something he'd say, "Hold on, darling, I know someone who can get that," and he'd get a number. He was right into it. I remember the Bonnie and Clyde look – cream beret, black pleated skirt, cream belt and stilettos – my dad loved it, he would say fabulous, he was a theatrical man himself. There was no discouragement for me and Laurie, it was like meeting like.'

There was so much to see and they soaked it all up. 'We'd watch Flamenco music to get the passion of it, go to reggae gigs or listen to Turkish music – there were little music bars on Goodge Street and Tottenham Court Road – or we'd go to the 100 Club to watch the old jazz players at 1 a.m.,' says Nikki. She considers his talent for dancing as integral to his skill as a footballer, not only were his balance and co-ordination improved by constant dancing, his mind was too. By rehearsing moves over and over again, he could visualise a sequence of moves in his head that his feet would automatically follow giving him a physical, as well as a mental, edge over opponents. I show her a photograph in which Cunningham is shown outpacing two opponents: he is at full stretch with his head turned to one side, his leading arm is extended and thrust forward away from his chest. Even in a still photograph the momentum, speed and power of the player is clear to see. Almost in silhouette Cunningham flashes between two harried defenders. She decodes it straightaway: 'That's a dance move, he's saying I've got a move; when you spend that much time with someone you begin to learn their body language. He's leading with his arm, he is going to go round and bring his foot back through his leg and jump and turn, it's like a dance sweep. We practised that for hours. We'd seen jazz dancers do it. His leading arm is pointing, you can tell by his hand the direction in which he is going to go, it's a gesture if you can read it. It used to make him laugh that they (opponents) couldn't see it. Everything was art to him, creative art, you could see it when he played.'

She was not the only person to define Cunningham in these terms. At the time the football writer Rob Hughes – an early advocate of Cunningham's and an admirer of Petchey's methods at Leyton Orient – described the young player in the following lyrical terms when he watched a training session on the waterlogged, muddy pitch at Brisbane Road: 'Laurie, a black teenager was inducing the soccer ball to rise, sway, bobble and spin. It roamed, seemingly at will, around his torso as Laurie flexed and arched like a limbo dancer. It was a dance of sorts. You could sense music – soul music

– throbbing to a rhythm in his mind, sense the brief touch of ball against chest, knee, foot. It climbed from instep to forehead, instep to forehead, then began rolling, rolling this way and that, shoulder to shoulder behind his neck. Laurie was lost in his art, man, lost.'

Allied to mesmerising control Cunningham was blessed with a rare suppleness. Thankfully his natural style had not been coached out of him at Orient, where he was rightly regarded as an unpolished gem who needed little instruction when it came to technical ability. His fitness was outstanding and his temperament, although at times wayward and brooding, was opening up to the mental and spiritual side of life and, in turn, the game. Although labelled a 'dreamer' or seen as sullen by some in the voluble environment of a professional football team, it was the ability to think independently and creatively that gave him his spark. He may not have said much in the dressing room but on the pitch his actions spoke loud and clear. He discovered that the mental and spiritual dimensions of life that he and Nikki explored, could also be expressed in his play. Football was as much a mental test as a physical one, and spoke directly to the mind-over-matter mantra the pair believed in when working out a complex dance move. Nikki describes his ability to 'levitate' while in mid-air. After he had jumped for a ball he had the ability to rise further and hang in the air – he could leap and 'add one more thing, it was weird', she observes. Rob Hughes noticed it too and after seeing him play for West Bromwich Albion in 1977 he asked, 'Have you seen a player, tightly marked, perform an exuberant aerial splits three feet off the ground and disturbing neither rhythm nor balance, flick the ball on behind him with the outside of his boot into a measured and enticing pass for his winger?' This balletic agility made Cunningham stand out, with the consequence that he became a target for the hatchet men that every First Division side seemed to possess at the time.

Off the field Cunningham may have felt like a marked man too. Sexual relationships between the races were still seen as taboo. As second-generation Caribbeans and white teenagers, who had grown up side by side in cities like London and Birmingham, started to go out together, newspaper editors and commentators wrote about a growing phenomenon – the mixed couple. With his stock rising on the pitch Cunningham began to enjoy an increasingly high profile off it. His eye-catching clothes and maverick personality singled him out as special and the fact that he had a glamorous white girlfriend made him a target for all those people who resented his lifestyle. Like all black players he received hate mail every week, but once it became known he was dating a white girl the volume of letters and poisonous phone calls increased. In a newspaper interview he reflected on the problem: 'I only wish it was that easy to convince all the people who send piles of abusive letters. I regularly get letters from the same people time after time. You'd think they would run out of ideas; most of them come up with novel methods to see me packed off to my home in some faraway jungle! The phone calls can get a bit naughty as well. Most of those anonymous "well-wishers" usually have a go at my white girlfriend Nikki, but we've been going out together for years so I don't think their advice is cutting much ice.' He says that both he and Nikki were inherently strong characters who could deal with the abuse and ends positively by concluding, 'I think more and more black and white couples will get together.'

Despite incidents like these, the years that Cunningham and Nikki were together, especially in London and Birmingham, were the most carefree of Cunningham's short life. The raw skinny kid from Finsbury Park, who found it as hard to focus as he did to get out of bed in the morning, had matured into a star in waiting. On the cusp of his move to West Bromwich Albion it seemed as if everything was going his way. Looking at photographs of Cunningham from this time the transformation in him is palpable. The working-class magpie who put together outfits from street markets and East End tailors on apprentice wages was stepping up in the world. His free-roaming style of play was an extension of the way he lived his life. Asked by a reporter what was the difference between white and black players, his simple reply was, 'They seem to attack the ball, we caress it.'

The couple shared an enthusiasm for dressing up for the occasion and loved to put on a persona. Nikki remarks, 'Life was like a film set for us ... we were forever studying, one day we were going to be psychologists so we would dress accordingly. We would go to lecture halls dressed as students and see what we could get into by our manner, dressing up and acting.' They were also striking to look at. Cunningham had grown into a handsome and stylish young man and Nikki with her long red hair and good looks immediately caught the eye. Leyton Orient player Bobby Fisher recalls one time when the team were booked on an early train at Euston station to travel to an away game and typically Cunningham was late. As the engine prepared to depart and doors were slammed shut Fisher presumed his friend had missed the train, but then he noticed two figures walking along the platform. He could tell it was his friend by his gait. The couple who so liked to imagine they were starring in their own film had become so convincing that they started to appear like that to friends. As they floated past the carriage window, he in a dove grey suit with a coat draped over his shoulders, she in a fur coat and long floral print dress, the chilly British Rail terminus was briefly invested with a moment of romance and glamour. The fact that he didn't think twice about bringing his girlfriend with him onto a train full of footballers showed where his priorities lay. Nikki says that what she loved about him most was an innocence that he never lost, but which was tested in their years together in Spain. 'If Laurie touched something it turned to gold with a different richness, not a financial richness ... a favourite saying of his was "different class". Even if something cost nothing or was genuine and he liked it, he'd say, "That's different class".'

By Autumn 1976 Cunningham's name was appearing in leading articles on the sports pages of the national press. Petchey banged the drum not only for Cunningham but for the exciting playing style favoured by black footballers as a whole when he challenged the *News of the World* to: 'Name me a better right winger. If all players were as talented there wouldn't be any need for coaches. I can't teach him anything, just watch him grow. The only way his talent is going to benefit is by experience. All the great internationals are picked when they're young. There's nothing in England that excites you like him. If he was selected it might inspire white players to invest in skill instead of aggression. If England qualify for Argentina [the 1978 World Cup finals, which they failed to do] we're going to need touch players. They will love him in South America and he'll be a tremendous asset.'

In the same article players and managers are canvassed for their opinion on Cunningham and their answers are a mix of the professionally non-committal and the banal, but a couple are worth noting. The usual opinions about black players are aired with perhaps the worst, most retrograde opinion coming from Clive Charles, himself a black player for Cardiff City who had recently been beaten by Cunningham's Leyton Orient in the league. He argues that black players are not good enough to represent England yet, suggesting it would be the worst thing possible for Cunningham to be given his full debut for the reason that if his 'tricks and wonders' were found wanting he would be dropped after just one game. Instead he proposes it would be better to wait another eighteen months before assessing him – the polar opposite to Petchey's view that all great players are picked when they are young. The implication from Charles is that Cunningham is a luxury player and therefore not to be wholly trusted.

Such a conservative attitude, suspicious of flair and mistrustful of skill for its own sake, was typical of football at the time. A pecking order of senior players meant exceptional youngsters sometimes had to wait for years to get a chance of being selected to play for their country. Former Liverpool player Brian Hall compared Cunningham to another young hopeful, Ray Wilkins at Chelsea. According to Hall, Cunningham's propensity to run with the ball showed a lack of maturity and suggested he needed to show a marked improvement to achieve anything compared to a more controlled type of player such as Wilkins whom he admired for his caution. Wilkins – a midfielder who went on to become a fulcrum of the England team and won eighty-four caps in the decade that followed – was known for his 'considered' style of play, and was nicknamed 'the Crab' by his detractors for his fondness for passing the ball sideways in the endless slow build-ups that characterised England performances at this time.

By December 1976 Cunningham's performances were good enough for him to expect a call-up to the England under-21 squad but he was left out by national manager Don Revie and Petchey could barely contain his anger telling reporters: 'It is obvious that Laurie is better than many of the squad and certainly has more experience. Perhaps the England manager hasn't watched Cunningham this season.' With a developing profile it was inevitable that Leyton Orient would start to receive offers from bigger clubs for Cunningham. By spring 1977, after a run of mediocre performances, the team were involved in a relegation battle and urgently needed £75,000 to pay off debts. The chairman had received an offer from the German side SV Hamburg for that amount if he agreed to the quick sale of Cunningham, but Petchey bridled. Believing his star player was worth more he dug his heels in. He knew he had a special player – as he had told anyone who would listen for the past five years – and wasn't going to belittle him by taking the first offer that came along. At the same time an old teammate called Ronnie Allen got in touch with Petchey. Allen was the assistant manager at West Bromwich Albion who were doing well in the First Division under their astute new manager Johnny Giles. Allen had heard that Cunningham was a terrific athlete and, by 1977, Petchey had finally got him to turn up on time as well. Giles invited player and manager to talk, with the caveat that £115,000 was a lot of money to pay for a player, to which Petchey offered the rejoinder, 'Yeah, and it's a lot of player.' After a preliminary chat Cunningham went to see Giles in his office but came out shortly after, telling Petchey, 'I ain't going to sign for them, they've only offered me £80 a week, I want £250. I won't go for less, I want to stay with you.' Petchey responded, 'Lol, if you come up here, you will get in the England team first time you play for them. Come on, you'll never play for England playing at bloody Orient. I'll go and see John.' Petchey told him what he thought the player was worth and Giles complained if he paid him £250 a week he would be their top player. Without missing a beat Petchey shot back, 'You're right, he will be your top player.'

Cunningham signed for West Bromwich Albion on 6 March 1977, two days before his twenty-first birthday, for a fee of £110,000. The five years he had spent at Orient under George Petchey were crucial to the making of him as a player. His thinking about the game improved dramatically as did his all-round reliability. He began to read the game with greater judgement, learning where to position himself, when to release the ball, when to hold on to it and when to run with it. As his game became more rounded so did his personality. The racism he experienced in the professional game – though unforgivable – improved his resilience and the hateful tackles aimed at him quickened his reflexes and perhaps made him more sure of himself. At Orient he was given a certain leeway to make mistakes and the support of a manager who knew he would learn from them. It also helped that whatever his boss told him kept coming true, so when Petchey said if he wanted to play for England he had to leave the club it was difficult to argue with him. The years between sixteen and twenty-one are pivotal for any young man, a time when individuality and identity are explored and developed. Cunningham was at the best place for him during these years, at a club where his unconventional personality was given the time and space to thrive. At another club he might have rebelled against the regime and dropped out of football altogether. Fortunately that did not happen, thanks largely to George Petchey, without whom the name Laurie Cunningham may never have been known.

5

RADICAL TO THE THIRD DEGREE

After twelve years at Don Revie's Leeds United – where, with Billy Bremner, he had come to personify that team's combination of skill and grittiness – Johnny Giles joined West Bromwich Albion as player-manager in 1975. The concept of player-manager was a relatively new one, and Giles, an eloquent Dubliner who at thirty-five hadn't many playing days left, was concentrating on managing in the next stage of his career. For Albion a figure of the stature of Giles, who could fulfil both roles of captain on the field and manager off it, appealed – as did his intelligence when speaking about the game. Giles arrived at a club that had known better days. Albion had a proud FA Cup pedigree, having won the competition on five occasions and been losing finalists the same number of times. But the halcyon days of the 1960s were long gone and in 1973 they were relegated to the Second Division. Giles modelled his playing style on the simple pattern that had worked so well at Leeds: steady, lateral build-up designed to keep the ball with him in the centre as ringmaster directing the play. And with some success – by spring 1976 Albion were pressing for promotion. In the game that secured it, away to Oldham Athletic, a *Sunday Times* match report asked if they were good enough to survive in the top division. It applauded the team's tight passing game but saw problems in attack where the target man Joe Mayo often mistimed his jumps or lacked the guile to shake off defenders: 'there is too little real skill up-front for them to trouble good defences.' Albion's first away game back in the First Division was against Giles's old side Leeds United at Elland Road where 40,000 fans gave him a hero's welcome, and they were unlucky not to win after conceding a ninetieth-minute equaliser that levelled the score at 2–2. Giles had created a hardworking, unified team that could surprise opponents on the break and, with players like Tony Brown bursting through from midfield or Willie Johnston hurtling down the wing, they were capable of causing damage to anyone. But Giles needed a quick-thinking player who had, as he put it, 'a little extra speed of reaction.'

Cunningham made his debut for Albion on 12 March 1977 against Tottenham at White Hart Lane. Albion won 2–0 and Cunningham played his part with a typical piece of skill when he casually shielded the ball by bouncing it on his thigh, angering his opponent so much that he kicked him and gave away a free kick from which Albion scored. On his home debut he scored against Ipswich Town and his tireless pace reportedly drew the exasperated cry from one gasping defender, 'For God's sake, slow down will you?' As a new face he had to impress a close-knit dressing room curious to know what £110,000 had bought them. Teammate John Trewick recalls, 'The first impression was that he was a bit arrogant. He came into the dressing room where we'd known each other for years and he was a bit aloof.' Giles had heeded the scouting reports of his assistant Ronnie Allen when he

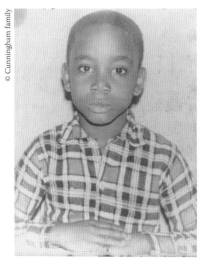

Laurie Cunningham.

The wedding of Elias and Mavis Cuningham, London, March 1958.

Highgate North Hill FC, *c.* 1968. Laurie is kneeling in the front row, third from right with the trophy in front of him.

Laurie Cunningham poses for the camera in his Leyton Orient kit, 1977.

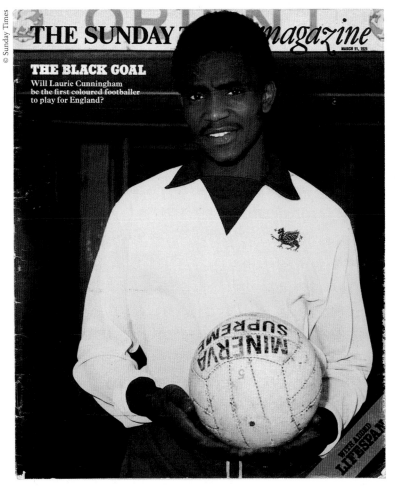

THE SUNDAY *magazine*

MARCH 21, 1976

THE BLACK GOAL

Will Laurie Cunningham
be the first coloured footballer
to play for England?

Cover of the *Sunday Times* magazine, 21 March 1976

Leyton Orient manager George Petchey with Laurie outside Leyton Orient FC, 2 February 1976.

Laurie Cunningham in action for Leyton Orient against Cardiff City.

Soul boys, with Dez Parkes in front, pose
outside 'Crackers' club in Soho, London,
August 1975.

Laurie shopping for clothes, *c.* 1976.

Exterior of the Black House, a hostel for homeless black teenagers at 571 Holloway Road, north London. The hostel was open between 1973 and 1977.

The back yard of the Black House on Holloway Road.

Laurie Cunningham's England debut, playing for the England under-21s against Scotland, 27 April 1977.

Laurie Cunningham in action againtst Southampton, 13 April 1979.

(*from left to right*) Laurie Cunningham, Brendon Batson and Cyrille Regis with US singing group the Three Degrees at the Hawthorns, home of West Bromwcih Albion, 1979.

Laurie meeting factory workers at the Smith Corona typewriter manufacturers, next door to the Hawthorns football ground, West Bromwich, April 1978.

Laurie with girlfriend Nikki Hare-Brown, July 1979.

Cyrille Regis (*left*) and Laurie look through photographs together, June 1978.

Mavis (*left*), Elias (*centre*) and Laurie Cunningham celebrate the news of his £950,000 transfer to Real Madrid, July 1979.

The leaving party held in Holloway, north London, for Laurie before his departure to Spain to play for Real Madrid. Included in the photograph are Mavis Cunningham, Cyrille Regis, Laurie Cunningham, Nikki Hare-Brown and Elias Cunningham, July 1979.

West Bromwich Albion director, John Gordon (*left*) and Laurie leave Heathrow
Airport together bound for Madrid, 29 July 1979.

Laurie Cunningham runs out for Real Madrid alongside team mate
Vicente Del Bosque at the Bernabéu stadium, Madrid, 9 September 1979.

Laurie Cunningham playing for England against Romania, 15 October 1980.

Laurie Cunningham in action for
Real Madrid.

Laurie playing for Real Madrid against
Barcelona at the Bernabéu Stadium,
23 September 1979.

Laurie and girlfriend Nikki in Madrid, *c.* 1980.

Laurie being escorted away from the Bernabéu stadium as an autograph hunter tries to grab his attention. Madrid, 9 September 1979.

Laurie shows his heavily scarred knee to the camera while undergoing medical treatment. Madrid, 25 October 1982.

Front cover of the sport section of the Spanish daily paper *ABC*, showing Laurie Cunningham as a cannibal, dancing around a pot that cooks Atletico Madrid manager Luis Aragones. Published 17 October 1983.

Flyer outside Rayo Vallecano football ground in Madrid, that shows Laurie wearing the Rayo Vallecano kit and reads: 'Love Rayo, Hate Racism'.

The English Heritage blue plaque outside Laurie's childhood home, 73 Lancaster Road in Finsbury Park, which was unveiled in September 2016.

Sergio and Silvia Sendin-Cunningham in Madrid June 2016.

signed Cunningham, but did not seem wholly persuaded by him, perhaps wary of his diffident nature. He seemed to confirm those doubts when commenting later on George Petchey's parting advice to keep talking to the young player: 'Laurie was a tremendously skilful player but I was not totally convinced about him. Orient were short of money and the deal was agreed.'

Albion were solid in defence and could play through the middle with attacking midfielder, and future England captain, Bryan Robson starting to impose himself on the team, and cult figure Willie Johnston on the left wing. Johnston, a Scottish international who had won the European Cup Winners' Cup with Glasgow Rangers in 1972, was a crowd-pleaser whose on-field antics included sitting on the ball and chatting to supporters at the corner flag. He had a flamboyant talent but a short fuse, and became infamous during the 1978 World Cup in Argentina when he was sent home after failing a drugs test. Shortly after joining Albion, Cunningham told Rob Hughes how Giles motivated him. 'He talks about Pelé. Johnny says what made Pelé, is he is the perfect pro; he does the simple things to the ultimate and saves the sensational stuff for goal scoring. I'm learning from that.' After a good start – he scored three goals in his first five appearances – he blotted his copybook by failing to turn up for training on the Monday morning before the following weekend's derby against Aston Villa. Most Saturday evenings he travelled back down to London, no doubt keen to get away from his Birmingham digs for the night, but the old indiscipline that had grudgingly been tolerated by Petchey was abhorred by Giles. 'I rang him at his home in London and he was still there. He said he had not come in because he had to go to the bank for his mother and do some other things. I was not interested. I told him I could not accept that. I had been brought up that you did not miss training at all; it is not right for your teammates to have this happen and his approach was that it was no problem, he was just so casual about it all.' Before any meaningful bond could develop between the two men Giles shocked everyone by announcing his resignation. He later explained that he felt constricted in his role and spoke of unhappiness at being overruled by the board on decisions about signings and player bonuses which he felt compromised his chances of success. 'Maybe I was looking for too much as a manager, but I am not dependent on the game that much for a living to accept anything less,' he announced in a farewell interview.

Ronnie Allen, Giles's assistant, was his replacement. A popular figure, he had been centre forward for Albion in the 1950s and also played for England. Although he didn't last a full season as manager, his most significant act just before he took over was to bring another black Londoner to the club when he advised Giles to buy Cyrille Regis, for an initial fee of £5,000 from non-league Hayes FC, after scouting him on the communal pitches at Regent's Park – the same pitches where Cunningham had played as a boy for Highgate North Hill a decade earlier. Allen was impressed with Regis's direct style of play and strength in the air: 'Regis is the best header of the ball I've seen since Jeff Astle.' Now no longer the only black player at the club, Cunningham enjoyed a chemistry with Regis off the pitch that soon became evident on it, as the team embarked on a barnstorming couple of seasons that brought national fame to the club and affection from fans and neutrals across the country. Regis, laid back and charismatic, was working as an electrician on building sites when Allen signed him. Born in French Guiana in 1958 his family arrived in London when he was five and eventually settled in Stonebridge Park in north-west London. Strong and fast as a teenager he could intimidate opponents with his size yet his sports teacher was most impressed by his temperament. 'You could have eaten anyone alive but nothing would anger you. It's one of the reasons you did so well as a professional footballer, you wouldn't let defenders get on top of you,' Regis writes in his autobiography, recalling his old teacher's words. Calmness was a characteristic he shared with Cunningham, although Regis, as a more gregarious figure, thrived on the humour and camaraderie of the dressing room. Growing up on the Stonebridge housing estate he listened to reggae music and followed his friend's sound system around London and lists his favourite artists as U-Roy, Dennis Brown and Augustus Pablo. Now in his late fifties, when we meet in a hotel bar in the centre of Birmingham, he still looks fit enough to pull on a shirt and play ninety minutes if required.

'We were nineteen and twenty-one years old, we thought we were mature, but we were not. It was my first year in the game. I was a reggae man, I loved the bassline, drinking Special Brew, eighteen-inch speakers, U-Roy and I-Roy. Laurie was a soul boy, his clothes were on a different level, almond-toed winkle-picker shoes, Yves Saint Laurent suits, silk shirts, he was very stylish going out in Birmingham, he took hours to get ready, he was like a woman ... press it, no, that don't look right, hours and hours. I've got to say he educated me, I just used to put on jeans and a tee shirt.'

Regis signed for Albion in May 1977 but carried on working on building sites for several weeks before joining the team in July: 'After going to Woolworth's in Harlesden, buying a dark red suitcase and packing all my things in it, I caught the train to Birmingham New Street.' He began in the reserves where he showed enough promise for Allen to quickly promote him to the first team for a League Cup tie against Rotherham United. Albion romped to victory and Regis crowned an energetic debut by scoring a penalty to the delight of the 15,000 crowd. He remembers the forward line that night was made up of himself, Cunningham and Willie Johnston, and the celebrations afterwards were an eye-opener compared to what he was used to at non-league Hayes. 'After the game we went to a pub fifty yards away from the ground called the Hawthorns. This is my debut. I'd come from non-League, we won 4–0 and we went straight there. I came out of there at 3 a.m. pissed as a rat, there were five or six of us, but Laurie wasn't there.' It wasn't until after the next game, at home to Middlesbrough in early September, that Regis and Cunningham became friends. The pair went out together, not to the pub, but to a wine bar. Regis says of his friend, 'He'd drink but not ten or twelve pints, he liked Mateus Rosé or Riesling – in those days it was wine bars, it was a bit more sophisticated, we went out to Rebecca's and that's how we got to know each other. He'd go out dancing with Nikki but I wasn't into all that. I'm a reggae man. I might do a few little steps but he'd be there dancing, even by himself. I was two years younger and we spent a lot of time together. I think the social aspect brought us together and that was a key element as to why we got on together on the pitch.'

By this time Cunningham was the most high-profile black footballer in the country after making his groundbreaking debut in an England shirt. He became the first black footballer to represent England professionally at any level when he was selected against Scotland in an under-21 game at Sheffield United's Bramall Lane on 27 April 1977. For many years it was thought Cunningham was the first black player to wear an England shirt outright, until 2013 when the Football Association acknowledged that Benjamin Odeje had played for England schoolboys in 1971. Cunningham had been tipped by the press as the player most likely to break the glass ceiling, most notably in a cover feature for the *Sunday Times Magazine* in March 1976. The article written by Brian Glanville titled 'The Great Black Hope' traced the history of black players in England and called for them to be picked for the national side. It criticised the myopia of many managers – 'our football today is pathetically full of sweat and effort and predictability' – and compared the development of English football unfavourably with that of Brazilian football, saying Brazil, 'who liberated their slaves only in 1888, were fully integrated on the football field by 1932. England by contrast still awaits her first black international cap ... Integration can only be complete when England awards a soccer cap to a black player.'

It seemed to be only a matter of time before a black player won international honours but progress was maddeningly slow. Cunningham's achievement on that Wednesday night in Sheffield in front of a sparse crowd of 9,000, drew plaudits from the daily papers (he scored the only goal in a nervy, untidy game) who saw in his performance evidence of a rare touch player. Colour footage of the match from Yorkshire TV misses the goal he scored but one sequence beautifully captures the allure of Cunningham in full flow. Somehow enhanced by the absence of commentary the film takes on the quality of a video installation and stands repeated viewing. Cunningham glides across the screen with the ball at his feet, swerving and feinting. He shows masterful control as he moves over a pitch mottled with divots and patches of sand. In a smooth-flowing, dipping run to the touchline that includes a step over, half-turn and full pirouette, he stops suddenly and rolls the ball back and forth under his foot, inviting his marker to lunge in, then a quick look up before slipping the ball to a teammate.

The *Daily Express* match report commented, 'You sensed the anticipation across the half-empty terraces each time Cunningham took possession in the second half, the kind of electricity that used to be generated by men like Jimmy Greaves', while the *Guardian* announced 'he looked a young man with a future'. In the same newspaper Frank Keating on the morning of the match previewed Cunningham's forthcoming debut with keen anticipation. Recalling the first time he had seen him at Leyton Orient, he wrote of the player's compelling presence: 'someone special had come amongst us', and quoted Arthur Rowe as saying, 'Tell you the truth, nothing much in our game now turns me on – but this boy Cunningham excites me more than anyone I can remember'. To Keating the significance of Cunningham appearing in the white shirt of England represented the fruition of a long, hard journey, 'The man–child who could lead the revolution that is so obviously coming, plays in an England shirt tonight ... he could well uncap a pressurised torrent of possibility in the British game. Cunningham could well set a celebrated seal on all the taunted, lonely pioneering work done down the years by the likes of Lindy Delapenha, Albert Johanneson, Roy Brown, Clyde Best, even Charlie Williams the comedian and one-time Doncaster defender. That lot and their long-forgotten friends, I warrant will raise a tiny cheer tonight wherever they are.'

And that cheer was raised and echoed by young blacks in the city of Sheffield. The night before the game Cunningham visited the Hub African–Caribbean centre on Sharrow Lane and stayed for a meal of rice and peas, chatting with youngsters as well as members of local amateur team Sheffield Caribbean FC. One of the players, Gilly Whyte, recalls the excitement when he discovered that Cunningham would be visiting. 'When we found out that Laurie was coming to the Hub we ran there from our training spot at Pomona Street, which was a two-mile sprint. When we saw him we were totally gobsmacked and didn't know what to say. He was a really pleasant guy. When he came to Sheffield, there were a lot more black guys who wanted to play football because of the visit. He was a hero to many.' Milton Samuels, the manager of Caribbean FC, cites the visit as his fondest memory in football: 'He was a role model. It can inspire young men, as they are not that far away from them. The lads who met him, they felt it was something they could aspire to. Laurie was a huge inspiration to young black people at the time. There were many highly talented black players in

Sheffield at the time of the visit, and though some forged professional careers there were a host of others who never fully realised their potential, and racism was a big factor in their underachievement.'

The importance of that night still resonates: it was at the Hub that the anti-racism charity Football Unites, Racism Divides was established in 1995 and continues to flourish today, albeit from new premises. *Rothman's Football Yearbook* named him in their First Division team of the year saying, 'because of the colour of his skin, Cunningham has had to put up with abuse from the ignorant section of the crowd, and provocation from opposing defenders. He has come through this test with flying colours so far – one only hopes that his progress in the game will be maintained.'

The Bramall Lane match was the first time Cunningham's parents had watched their son in action. His father Elias said that he did not fully understand the rules but enjoyed seeing his son score the winning goal, and his mother Mavis spoke of her pride and joy in seeing her 'England boy' wearing the famous white shirt. For Michael La Rose, his teammate from Highgate North Hill who was used to black players furthering their careers abroad or drifting away from the game entirely, Cunningham playing that night was a special victory: 'It was a very important moment for me as a black person in Britain. Black players were more than up to it. I was surprised that Laurie broke through at England level even though he was showing that ability, because there was a distrust of flair players, and true to fact, at senior level it was Viv Anderson who got through because he was a sturdy, solid northern defender.'

A month later Cunningham experienced shocking racism while on tour with England at an under-21 tournament in Finland. Given an evening off by boss Les Cocker, a group of players went to the local cabaret and Cunningham, who had to be cajoled by room-mate John Richards to go, was stopped by a bouncer at the door who grabbed him by the shoulder and said, 'The white guy can come in, but you stay outside'. Both players pointed to the badges on their jackets indicating they were part of the England team but in response the bouncer pointed to Cunningham's face and shook his head. Cunningham received words of encouragement after the incident from the leader of the FA party, Sir Matt Busby, who told reporters, 'Laurie is acutely conscious of his colour, but his problems are in his own hands. He knows he has the ability to be a world-class player. If he can win his personal battle he will do good for every coloured person in England. He has amazing talent and he reminds me of the young Pelé. He has the same rhythm and movement and the skill, grace and control to follow him … Laurie has unusual courage and I believe this tour will have done him good because it has spelled out the difficulties … Laurie will have to live on his skill and as long as he can do that, no other considerations will affect his international future.'

Back in the First Division, Albion had finished seventh and Cunningham ended the season with six goals in thirteen matches. New manager Allen recognised the potential of his black players while being aware of the barriers they faced: 'There would be even more coloured lads playing, but many professional soccer scouts are prejudiced by old-fashioned theories. There is a widely held belief that coloured players lack aggression and courage. Cunningham and Regis have the ideal temperament. They walk away smiling and know the best way of answering ignorance and rudeness is with their own ability.' A few weeks into the new season, on the August Bank Holiday weekend, Cunningham's resilience was put to the test when Albion travelled to Anfield to face Liverpool. Mark Leech, a young sports photographer at the time, covered the match because Kenny Dalglish had recently signed for the club as replacement for Kevin Keegan. Lying face down in position at The Kop end in front of 20,000 fans, he was keen to capture the new signing attacking the home end but soon became fascinated with the contest that developed between Cunningham on the right wing and Liverpool left back Joey Jones. Jones was highly regarded by the home fans; a hard-tackling Welshman with a Liver Bird tattooed on his forearm, he was adored for his full-blooded, uncompromising performances. His cult status had been enhanced in the European Cup Final earlier that year where Liverpool beat Borussia Mönchengladbach in Rome and a memorable banner was unfurled by fans that read, 'Joey ate the frogs legs, made the swiss roll, now he's munching gladbach'. As a contest the duel was a contrast of styles, Cunningham the swift and tricky young winger versus Jones the hard-tackling European Cup winner playing in front of a gallery who idolised him. Jones got in early with a couple of high tackles and continued to push it to the limit as he went unpunished by the referee – while Cunningham's pace and sudden forward spurts made him difficult to pin down, especially from behind a lens. Leech comments, 'Back then you didn't have ten frames a second cameras, you had to pick your shot, and Cunningham threw me because you didn't know where he was going. He's there and then he's gone. You think he's coming inside and he goes outside. I can't really look at my archive and say I've got the shot of Cunningham that I really nailed him.'

Cunningham endured a difficult afternoon that was not helped when he went to take a corner and the home fans burst into a chorus of 'Hello, dere man, hello, dere man' in cod minstrel voices – *The Black and White Minstrel Show* where white singers blacked-up to sing songs such as 'The Camptown Races' was popular at the time and had been a TV variety staple for over twenty years. The Kop nonetheless loved the duel between the two players. Leech says, 'You had a super lad coming to Anfield trying to make a mug out of Joey Jones, a player who was a lot less skilful, and he used what he had in the book to stop him.' As the tackles flew in and the jeers got louder each time he touched the ball, Allen substituted Cunningham, perhaps for his own safety and he left the pitch to chants of 'Where's you nigger now?' ringing in his ears. The competition was over for the day and Liverpool ran out 3–0 winners.

When I ask Cyrille Regis how Cunningham dealt with such abuse, he says: 'Like most of us did. Sometimes you get angry and think what the hell's going on, which is natural. Of course you might react to the crowd but in the main you take on that negative reaction and push it out into performance. You think, how can I hurt you back? You try harder. That's what we did, we didn't go home and cry about it.' Regis coped by rationalising the situation as one that was specific to match day. 'You worked out it only happened in the arena where you could do something about it. No one was calling you nigger outside of the game, five thousand might do inside, those people would probably talk to you if they saw you out and about.'

Lord Ouseley, the chairman of Kick It Out, the anti-discrimination football charity, remembers standing on the terraces at Stamford Bridge watching Cunningham play for Albion against Chelsea. He recollects how he picked up the ball on the halfway line and dribbled at pace towards goal before smashing it into the top corner from the edge of the box. One individual was impressed enough to say out loud to the man standing next to him, 'These niggers can play.' Michael La Rose points out that many London clubs had a sizeable black fan base, in particular Arsenal and Tottenham, reflecting the multi-racial make-up of those areas. It's his belief that racism was at its most damaging and entrenched within those clubs themselves which rejected black players as schoolboys and were unwilling to nurture their talent because of the fallacy that they were cowardly. He remembers being uncomfortable watching football matches: 'You were always aware you had to be careful because the firms – hard-core fans intent on violence – would target any black person in the crowd. In the Shed [the home end] at Chelsea they used to wear these overalls, brown butcher's coats. West Ham tended to be older men, dockers with hammers and chains for violence. I remember thinking I'm glad I'm on this side, the West Ham side ... they were very racist; the Chelsea fans were younger and the leader of the Chelsea firm was a black guy, so that tells you about the complexity of race, the complexity of the emerging Britain. Chelsea booed their own black players but West Ham didn't. That's the complexity of it.'

Cunningham put it simply and with more dignity than his tormentors when he gave a succinct appraisal of himself and his situation: 'I haven't got a fiery temper and maybe that helps because I'm able to walk away from explosive situations. It takes a lot to get me to lose my rag and so far I've been more interested in getting on with the game than looking for trouble. It's always better to keep cool and maintain your concentration otherwise you can be a menace to yourself and the rest of the team. Since arriving in the Midlands and the First Division I've been conscious of the encouragement we can generate among black kids in the area. A lot of nonsense has been talked about black players not having enough heart for the game when the going gets tough. Well that's a theory that has been quickly dispelled. More black players are coming into the game all the time and that can only help others to try their luck. I want to tell a lot of these black kids out there that the same thing can happen to them.'

The problem of racial chanting at grounds was occasionally noted in newspapers but nobody seemed prepared to do much about it. No one was ever thrown out of a ground for it or even cautioned by stewards or the police. Clubs preferred to treat it as a social problem that was beyond their remit. Many football grounds were in a poor state of repair. Despite huge attendances at First Division matches, grounds had rudimentary facilities with rusting, creaking stands and basic concrete terracing. Prices were affordable – but very little of that money went on maintenance and repairs, the money went straight into the pockets of the directors who didn't see the need to spend money on extra police or training programmes for stewards. The only way to put an end to abuse was to field more black players; the more that took to the pitch the more difficult it became to chant against them, particularly if one was playing for your team.

Albion began the 1977–78 season well enough; they were third by mid-October and Allen was full of praise for his black strikers. 'They have brought a breath of fresh air to our football,' he beamed – but a dramatic slump in form followed shortly after. Cunningham hit a lean spell and a series of anonymous performances led to him being dropped. The bright start of his early games in the spring became a fading memory as the end of the year approached. Defeat in the League Cup by Third Division Bury and a poor run of results in December led to talk of a mid-season crisis.

Matters were made worse when Allen suddenly announced he was leaving the club. Albion had played an exhibition match in Saudi Arabia and Jimmy Hill, the former player and TV pundit, acting as fixer for a business consortium that arranged football appointments in the Kingdom, approached Allen with the offer to manage the national team for £100,000 tax-free. Allen accepted on the spot and terms were quickly agreed. The astonishing offer, for only sixteen months' work, could not, of course, be matched by Albion and club captain John Wile was appointed caretaker manager while the board looked for a new man.

In an eventful nine months, Cunningham had signed for Albion, made his debut for England, been named in the First Division team of the season, been relegated to the bench and seen two managers leave the club. Wile, a mainstay of the Albion defence and a natural leader, later remembered in Dave Bowler and Jas Bains's book *Samba in the Smethwick*

End, 'Laurie was a one-off in lots of things – the way he played, his dress sense. He didn't find mixing with other people easy and at times he didn't endear himself to the rest of the players because he did act as an individual when we were very much a group. Laurie would be late for training, he stretched things a bit, which went against the grain, he had his own ideas and sometimes that didn't make him too popular. It never became a big problem but it did upset people now and again.' As the year drew to a close the goodwill was in danger of dissipating as Albion dropped down the table and Cunningham struggled to regain form.

Three weeks after Allen's departure in January 1978, Albion appointed thirty-seven-year-old Ron Atkinson as manager on a three-year contract. Atkinson, who had got Cambridge United promoted from the Fourth Division as champions and into a challenging position in the Third Division, was confident he was coming to a club with the potential to take on the top teams in the country. Giles and Allen had bequeathed him a talented squad of players. A gifted man-manager with a memorable turn of phrase, his self-belief and charm went a long way towards raising the profile of the club. The press loved his bravado (and full-length leather trenchcoat) when he claimed he was ready to break the northern clubs' stranglehold on the major trophies. The Midlands had suffered for years in comparison to London and the North when it came to coverage of its football teams, with the Black Country in particular characterised as a bleak industrial backwater that had barely modernised since Victorian times and which produced sturdy, bread-and-butter football teams. The London press covered the big clubs in the capital and those in Manchester and Liverpool, while the Midlands' teams were stuck with a terminally unglamorous image. However, the success of teams such as Nottingham Forest, Aston Villa and West Bromwich Albion in the next few years saw the beginning of a golden age and a period of success which brought kudos to the region that had been missing for years. At the forefront of this change of image, from grit to glamour, were the swashbuckling figures of Cunningham and Regis, playing an irresistible brand of football that was to capture the imagination of fans everywhere.

Atkinson's lone signing on his arrival was his captain at Cambridge, Brendon Batson, whom he brought to the club for a fee of £30,000. Like Regis, Batson spent his early childhood in the Caribbean. He was born in Grenada in 1953 then moved to Trinidad for a brief period before coming to England aged nine years old in 1962. He grew up in Tilbury in Essex, the estuary town where the *Empire Windrush* had docked fourteen years earlier, and it was here that he first played football, at school, then later for the district, where in time he was scouted by Arsenal. Like Cunningham he trained twice a week at Highbury but he was kept on and offered a professional contract when he was seventeen. Less the maverick and more a dependable team player, his talent as a smooth defender with an exemplary attitude appealed to Arsenal, who saw the potential in a proud, self-confident young man. After making his debut at the age of eighteen he struggled to establish himself in the senior team and, faced with a future on the fringes, he requested a transfer and in 1974 joined Third Division Cambridge United.

Cunningham's loss of form, meanwhile, was puzzling. His experiences with the England under-21s had seemed to dent his confidence rather than improve it. The more he strived the less he seemed to succeed. Cyrille Regis believes, 'He, like a number of highly talented players, suffered from inconsistency. When you are highly talented people want that every day and if they don't get it they'll start doubting and run with someone less talented but more consistent. Laurie would excel in some games but in others he'd give you five out of ten and that frustrates managers, it frustrates people.' He continues, 'The dressing room is a place of work. You don't have to like everybody but you establish a working relationship. Laurie was reserved, some could see it as aloof, but he wasn't that personality, he was on his guard until he got to know you.'

Shortly after his appointment Atkinson called his player in for a clear-the-air session with his teammates in an attempt to find out why his form had dipped so badly. An article in *World Soccer* magazine described Cunningham as 'very much a "loner" inasmuch that he does not mix a great deal with the other players. This is one point he had to stress to his colleagues because they could not understand his reluctance to take part in the activities aimed at selling West Bromwich Albion to the general public.' It goes on to quote Cunningham: 'they couldn't understand that I am ill at ease in such circumstances. There is nothing personal against the other players but they couldn't understand me until we had this meeting ... There is now a better understanding between myself and the rest of the players at the Albion. This is helping me because I feel a great deal more settled than when I first arrived.' In an away match against Ipswich Town, Atkinson's third game in charge, the players who would later become known as 'the Three Degrees' played together for the first time, with Cunningham coming on as substitute to partner Regis in attack, with Batson at right back. Albion's season continued with a run in the FA Cup that ended in defeat in the semi-final, but a late reversal in league form and a string of wins saw them finish in sixth place, which, with Liverpool winning the European Cup, was good enough for them to qualify for the UEFA Cup. As he looked back on the season Cunningham must have realised he had been a peripheral figure in a disappointing campaign. His five goals in thirty-two games compared badly to his six in thirteen the season before, yet there were signs of hope: he had found a close friend in Cyrille Regis, he felt less isolated than when he had first moved to Birmingham after joining Albion, the managerial upheavals of the past year were resolved, and a young, charismatic boss who loved to see attacking football from his players was in place. With a good start the coming season promised an extended run in the team with the added glamour of European competition.

Before that could happen the squad were taken on an unusual summer tour of China by chairman Bert Millichip. Millichip, who was also a senior figure at the Football Association, had seized the opportunity after a combined tour and trade mission organised for the England team by the FA had fallen through. The team spent three weeks in the country playing exhibition matches and attending cultural events. A BBC film crew for the documentary series *The World About Us* followed them around and the resulting programme, *Albion in the Orient*, was broadcast in September 1978. In it Cunningham appears a diffident background presence; in one long shot all three black players are filmed walking apart from their colleagues, perhaps to suggest a division in the camp, but, as Cyrille Regis explains, this was far from the truth. The whole squad were cooped up and felt constrained by the way they were expected to behave: 'We were bored so went everywhere we could. There were no pubs. All we had to do were the cultural things, we couldn't wait to get to Hong Kong. With a twenty-year-old head on you, you want birds, you want pubs, not to be on your best behaviour. I'd love to do it now at my age. This was communist China; you couldn't go to certain areas. We played seven exhibition games over three weeks so there was a lot of boredom.'

Boredom provoked sarcasm and the most memorable line from the documentary was uttered by midfielder John Trewick who, after yet another stultifying day of culture, looked a defeated man as he sat in front of the Great Wall of China and commented glumly, 'Once you've seen one wall you've seen them all.' The games, played before huge but curiously silent crowds, were not only useful as bonding exercises but were important in bringing the Three Degrees together on the field. Brendon Batson became first choice as right back, Cyrille Regis continued as centre forward and, in the absence of Willie Johnston, on World Cup duty for Scotland in Argentina, Cunningham was given free rein on either wing in matches. The experience of travelling, living and even being bored together in a strange country had a positive effect on the players. The trade benefits may remain unknown but the renewed confidence and camaraderie engendered in the Albion team was invaluable.

After eight months in charge Atkinson finally settled on his starting line-up. The team had been taught by Johnny Giles to play a calm, economical passing game, which he did not interfere with but insisted his players push forward and attack at every opportunity. Underpinned by a powerful back four, with John Wile and Ally Robertson in central defence, Brendon Batson at right back and young Derek Statham, one of the most promising left backs in the country, providing the foundation, this was a team that from the midfield up was filled with marauding talent such as Bryan Robson and Tony 'Bomber' Brown, and spearheaded by Cyrille Regis and Laurie Cunningham. Regis recalls, 'We were given that freedom, the structure was in place behind us. 4–4–2, this is how we play. Structure comes when you are defending, when you are attacking it's instinct, you go for something, no one teaches you to do it, it's down to you to make decisions. Going forward is creativity – that's why we love football ... Laurie went on either wing, if he was having a good game against a left back he'd stay there, if not he'd switch. We were such a fluid side that Laurie just went everywhere and we were such great friends that we'd work things out, talk about it when we were out, "You do this and I do that, look over my shoulder and pass it there," we used to talk about things, all of a sudden it clicked.'

In Regis, Cunningham had found someone with whom he felt completely relaxed and who enabled him to play in the free-flowing, natural style that he loved. It's notable too how Regis appears to echo the words of Robert Johnson,

Cunningham's good friend and teammate throughout his teenage years. Regis is also quick to point out that he personally benefited from the experience of his fellow centre forward Ally Brown: 'He was superb for me as a young kid, he told me where to run and when to hold it up. We had a fantastic side!' Albion won the first five games of the new season and opened their UEFA Cup campaign by beating Turkish side Galatasaray. The good start was reflected in Cunningham's improved goal tally – he scored four in seven games – and in October they treated the Hawthorns to a 7–1 thrashing of Coventry City, with Cunningham scoring twice. The improved form was not the result of a radical change in tactics, which played little part in team preparation. Regis recalls, 'We weren't coached, there were no set rules. We'd play twenty minutes of high tempo five-a-side, a bit of crossing and shooting, some stomachs and sprints, pub by 12.30. Everybody did it, Liverpool did it, we did it, it wasn't until the early eighties that coaching came in. It was always five-a-side; there was a little bit of a rebellion at West Brom when coaching came in.' And Atkinson energised the training ground in his own unique way. In *Samba in the Smethwick End*, midfielder Tony Brown is quoted as saying, 'Ron Atkinson ... brings out the best in everyone. It's the same with a five-a-side game in training when he backs his team called "English Cream" against what he terms "Foreign Scum". He really gets the lads going! ... The approach is right. I've never enjoyed myself so much in all my life.' Presumably the 'foreign scum' were any Scots, Welsh or Irishmen in the squad.

Cunningham had grown in confidence and experience and adapted his game to protect himself from the more punishing

First Division defenders. Criticised by some for gilding the lily too often, in an illuminating interview with the *Sun* he talked about what he had learnt. Early in his career he often played on after hard, damaging tackles to prove that he was no coward – 'instead of staying down and getting treatment I'd pick myself up and carry on' – and recalls a game against Newcastle United in 1977 shortly after joining Albion where he came unstuck. Albion were winning 3–0 and by his own admission he was 'getting a bit too cocky'. 'I picked up the ball just inside their half and went off on a run. I could see a couple of their lads coming across to cut me off, but I managed to slip the tackles. It was then I heard the St James' crowd groan. They knew what was coming and too late I saw a third defender bearing down on me. I realised in that split second that I'd overdone it. And the tackle confirmed my worst fears. No names – but that player knows the damage. I was out for nearly a month with severely damaged ligaments. But again I learned from that bitter experience ... that Newcastle incident taught me not to overdo the mickey-taking.'

The approaching winter of 1978 saw two of the definitive Albion games from this period, still talked about whenever fans recall the golden era of the Three Degrees at the Hawthorns. The first showed how far Albion had come under Atkinson. A unified and effective team, they now had the flair and confidence to meet the best in Europe on equal terms with a fearless attitude and adventurous spirit that reached its apogee when they played the first leg away to Valencia in the third round of the UEFA Cup that November.

Valencia were a top side at the time and an experienced European outfit who were one of the favourites to win the competition outright, and had the talismanic Argentinian striker Mario Kempes. Kempes had been voted player of the tournament in the World Cup finals the previous summer and also won the Golden Boot. The game finished 1–1, with Albion scoring a valuable away goal, but it was the nature of the performance that surprised many. Albion endured waves of early pressure and conceded after seventeen minutes; soon after, two desperate tackles by John Wile and Brendon Batson kept their chances alive, but as the storm passed they gradually established a dominance over the home team that became unstoppable. Instead of playing safe Albion went on the offensive: in midfield they were first to the ball and looked sharper and quicker than their more illustrious opponents. At half-time Atkinson told his men that if there was a ball to be won, win it, and urged his players, full backs included, to continually exert pressure to keep Valencia pegged back.

The strategy paid off three minutes into the second half when Ally Brown beat two defenders, went to the byline and pulled the ball back to the six-yard box where Cunningham raced in to beat the prone goalkeeper to the ball and smash home the equaliser. The *Daily Mirror* reported: 'There will not be a better goal scored anywhere this season than the one Cunningham got in the forty-eighth minute'. The second half was now Albion's for the taking and Cunningham rose to the occasion, playing probably his best game for the team. Cyrille Regis recalls: 'Laurie was phenomenal, he tore them apart'. Albion should have scored again but desperate defending, goalmouth scrambles and the Spanish goalkeeper, Pereira, stopping a twenty-yard effort with his face, kept the scores level as the referee blew for full-time. In a post-match interview striker Ally Brown said, 'We played 'em off the park, didn't we?' while Cunningham chipped in with 'Bloody great!'

Headlines the next morning raved about his display: 'El Cunningham is the Hero', 'Cunningham the Master' and 'The Black Pearl'. The *Daily Mirror* had a dig at Kempes, supposedly the best player in the world, saying, 'He was made to look a second-rate selling player here by the silky skills of a skinny black kid from London.' The *Daily Express* was equally as enthusiastic – 'a performance of breathtaking skills from the twenty-two-year-old Londoner' – and the *Sun* concluded their match report by echoing Ron Atkinson's comparison of his player to George Best: 'It was no more than Albion and the Black Best of English soccer deserved.' Even the Valencia fans gave Albion a standing ovation as they left the pitch, the *Guardian* noting, 'The home supporters were showing their appreciation for Albion's attacking football in general and Cunningham's performance in particular. It was gratifying to see a foreign crowd rising to English players in the same way that British crowds have responded to Cruyff, Eusébio, Puskás, Di Stéfano, Gento and so on. Cunningham has yet to reach those standards, but as Ron Atkinson, the West Bromwich manager, said: "He couldn't get enough of the ball for the Valencia fans."'

The match was broadcast live on Spanish television and provided the perfect showcase for Cunningham to announce his brilliance to the clubs of Europe, including the most celebrated of them all, Real Madrid. In the return fixture a fortnight later, on a typically raw Black Country night, Albion won 2–0 but could easily had scored more after hitting the bar and post and having two goals disallowed. Cunningham won praise from his manager for creating the second goal, calling the move that created it, 'a combination of speed, skill and opportunism. Pure magic.'

The second thrilling match of that winter of 1978 was played against Manchester United a month later in December. United were no longer the force they had once been and were a club in transition after the era of Best, Law and Charlton had come to an end but were still a formidable prospect on home turf at Old Trafford. The game was televised and the commentator Gerald Sinstadt set the scene with an impromptu weather bulletin before kick-off when he reported 'the air temperature on the ground is just above freezing'. As the camera cuts away to a chilled Old Trafford it shows men standing side by side in anoraks with caps and scarves and looks a good deal colder. A lone black supporter in a white bobble hat is briefly visible among the masses and he probably knew what to expect as Albion's three black players took to the field.

Throughout the match Cunningham, Regis and Batson are subjected to 'the treatment' – jeering monkey calls every time they touched the ball. The camera lingers on Cunningham for a moment before kick-off and Sinstadt observes, 'For Albion their adventurous style this season owes much to Laurie Cunningham.' As the game gets underway sunlight briefly brightens the littered, wind-blown pitch as flurries of snow drift to the ground. Despite the unpromising conditions and hostile atmosphere the game – which finished 5–3 to Albion, and has seen six goals by half-time – is (as the scoreline suggests) open and attacking and a joy to watch, with both teams scoring excellent goals. Albion are devastatingly fluid and perform with a confidence and control that is hard to stop; the anticipation and movement throughout the team on a darkening Manchester afternoon is beautiful to watch even forty years later. Albion could easily have scored seven but for United goalkeeper Gary Bailey making two world-class saves, and the goals they score are all well-crafted team goals of the highest quality.

For the first Cunningham picks up the ball on the left wing and is immediately barracked by the crowd with monkey noises audible enough to be caught on TV. Sinstadt remarks, 'The booing of the black players … ' but before he can finish his sentence is interrupted as Cunningham passes to Tony Brown on the edge of the area who meets it first time with a sudden curling left-foot shot and scores. Sinstadt recovers well to finish his sentence ' … the booing is repaid by Tony Brown, Cunningham booed there but unperturbed.' It is clear the 'booing' is in fact monkey noises. Later in the game, when he takes a throw-in, Cunningham is once again subjected to the same noises but this time the 'booing' goes unremarked.

The second goal starts with Cunningham picking up the ball in midfield and beating two players before passing it to Cyrille Regis on the edge of the box. With a deft back-heel, Regis sets up Len Cantello, coming in at full pelt, who thumps the ball into the net. Cunningham scores the fourth after a straight as a gun barrel run towards goal leaves two trailing defenders on their backsides; but the best is saved for last as a neat passing move is completed with a flick from Ally Brown to set up a marauding Cyrille Regis, who sweeps himself off his own feet, such is the power of the strike, as he smashes the ball into the roof of the net from an acute angle.

Sinstadt screams with delight, 'Oh, what a great goal! What a magnificent goal!'

A few days later Cunningham was voted footballer of the month by the *Evening Standard*, who called Albion 'the team for 1979' and enthused, 'The terraces at the Hawthorns are alive with the possibility of the club landing the title for the first time in fifty-nine years. Overnight, it seems, the team is stacked with superstars – iron man defender John Wile, the powerful Regis, the goal-crazy Ally Brown and Tony Brown and the midfield cunning of Len Cantello. But if you seek excitement look no further than Cunningham. He is the youngster warming the crowds most with a combination of speed, hard shooting and skill.' Albion's blistering run of form had seen them top the league early in January 1979 and the new year was full of promise.

Unfortunately it brought harsh, unrelenting winter weather which froze the Hawthorns for several weeks, making the pitch unplayable. In six weeks, from the middle of January to the end of February, Albion played just one game – an away match at Anfield – as the momentum of the preceding months was stopped in its tracks by the severity of the cold snap. The fixture pile-up proved disastrous for Albion's title chances. When the weather finally relented the backlog of matches meant Albion had to play twenty-five games in just over two months, and, as game after game began to take its toll on the small squad of players, an enervated side struggled to keep going. Cyrille Regis recalls one away game: 'We went to Bristol and lost because we couldn't move, we were just absolutely shattered.' In April, confidence was tested as Albion drew five games in a row and lost one, and as the season came to its conclusion, Liverpool, who had benefited from undersoil heating at Anfield in the freezing weeks, became champions with Albion finishing third, after being pipped to runners-up spot by Brian Clough's Nottingham Forest. The bad luck carried over into cup competitions too; within the space of two weeks Albion were knocked out of the FA Cup by Southampton and beaten in the UEFA Cup by Red Star Belgrade, after a late equaliser in the second leg put the Yugoslavian side through on away goals – a ruthless physical performance having negated the home side. The bright start which promised so much had, like the snow and ice, melted away to nothing and Albion finished the season without a trophy and the unenviable tag of a 'nearly club'.

The smooth bravado of Albion's best performances won over many neutrals and the combination of Cunningham and Regis up front made an impact still present to this day. For Regis simplicity was the key to their success. Atkinson knew his strikers would create chances and that they possessed a rare understanding that helped them make the right decisions on the pitch, so he told them to just go out and entertain him, the manager. "'If I'm getting entertained the fans are getting entertained," he said. He loved to let us go and play, he'd say go and express yourself, not do this, do that, he'd whisper in our ear, "Go and excite me." Recognition came from the Professional Footballers' Association when both players were nominated for Young Footballer of the Year for 1978. At the awards dinner held at the Grosvenor House Hotel in London, Regis and Cunningham were sitting together at the nominees table in evening dress as Kevin Keegan announced the winner from the stage. Regis was surprised, and felt mildly guilty, when he heard his name called: 'Three-quarters of my goals were Laurie crossing them in from the wing, it was a bit embarrassing. I got the award but Laurie was creating the goals for me.' He was swiftly brought down to earth when his teammate greeted his return to the table with the words 'cheesy twat!'.

The award was an impressive achievement given that Regis had only been playing professionally for a year, and showed how respected Albion had become as a team. Batson, Regis and Cunningham had reminded coaches and fellow players that black footballers had brains. The trio's photogenic good looks stood out and the impromptu nickname 'the Three Degrees' (a popular American group of the day), coined by the ever quick-witted Atkinson, caught on as press interest in the players spread. Regis remarks on the enduring status of the three of them when he says, 'To see black players in the mud and the snow was inspirational. Ian Wright told me "You and Laurie are my heroes." Laurie was much better on the eye than me, I was more power and strength; Laurie was beautiful on the eye, honestly he was so graceful, he was on his toes. The Three Degrees captured the second generation's imagination: if they can do it, I can do it ... It's only when you look back you think that was amazing. There were quite a few black players playing but they weren't in the First Division so didn't get the exposure. When you are on *Match of the Day*, it's radical. There was hardly anything with black people on television so when we were on it was radical.' He adds, 'You're not conscious of history; there was no way we were conscious of the effect we were having on the psyche of young black men, not even just black men, but black people – they were proud. Loads of black women say to me, "Cyrille Regis, I remember you, man, I used to watch you on the television," and they are in their sixties, seventies, eighties, but they can remember watching me on television.'

Cunningham probably didn't realise how well-known he had become, and if he did, it didn't seem to affect his modest nature. On one trip back to London he bumped into an old friend from his soul boy days, Steve Salvari. He recalls: 'I was walking up Oxford Street and I heard this big whistle, and of course it's Laurie, and he's got this tall fella with him. He came running across the road. By this time he was a big star and he ran over with this bloke and says, "Steve man, how are you? This is Cyrille by the way." As if I din't know! He didn't make any assumptions at all. He was asking about everybody because he obviously wasn't around as much as he used to be, and Cyrille knew all about us lot. We just stood there chatting for twenty minutes or so, and it was as if no time had passed at all.'

In May 1979 an unusual game took place at the Hawthorns that showed how much the Three Degrees had come to be the public face of Albion. A couple of weeks after the general election that saw Margaret Thatcher swept to power, and in which the National Front had fielded more than 300 candidates, a testimonial match was held for long-serving midfielder Len Cantello where an All Black XI played against an All White XI. The White XI were made up of members of the Albion squad (former manager Johnny Giles also lined up) while the Black XI, or 'Regis and Cunningham XI' as it was billed, consisted of an invitational side of black players from across the leagues, among them Garth Crooks of Stoke

City, and Bob Hazell and George Berry of Wolves. It was the first time the country's top black players had come together outside their clubs and many had never even met before.

Ron Atkinson opened the evening's football with his own XI playing against the 'local press and TV personalities XI'. Although the idea of a Black versus White game may seem crass today, the match was played in the right spirit, with players showboating and turning on the training-ground tricks for the 7,000 fans who had turned out. In an era when racial abuse was the norm, the multiracial crowd were thoroughly entertained and able to watch a match without having to listen to the monkey chants and boos that were usually heard whenever a black player touched the ball inside a football ground. The black historian and academic Paul Gilroy, who moved to Birmingham in 1978, was at the game and says the whole idea of the match intrigued him and his friends. When they heard about it their first thought was 'Black vs White, I've got to see that.' 'There was a big black Handsworth Brummie contingent at that game … Laurie was a hero at the time, I've got this memory of him taking a corner and it was a work of art, it was sublime, he always had so much time … the man was a complete footballer.' For the record the All Black side won the match 3–2.

Cunningham's calm disposition meant he rarely retaliated to verbal abuse during a game but when it happened face-to-face away from the pitch, the pressure to react must have been overwhelming. Nikki recounts one incident when her boyfriend lost his cool. After a night out in Birmingham they were approaching a cab office to order a car home, and as they passed three men, one shouted out, 'Nigger loving slag!' The couple continued for a few steps until Cunningham muttered, 'That's the one!' She continues, 'I said keep walking, but he said, "No, its too late," and he turned and faced them. One of them went in for a head-butt and I screamed. Laurie being so "Kung-Fu" moved and used the man's strength against him to put him on the ground. Meanwhile I ran into the minicab office crying "Help! Help!" and they came out, but by then he had all three of them on the ground. Laurie said, "You see! you see! Now apologise to her." And it was done and dusted.' The violence of the situation was not without a comic moment when one of the assailants got back to his feet with the startled realisation, 'Oh my God! It's Laurie Cunningham, I bloody love you.'

On 23 May 1979, Cunningham won his first senior England cap in a Home International tournament match against Wales at Wembley. The match was goalless but was recognition, at last, of the promise he had shown over the past two seasons, and the popular impact of the Three Degrees was made clear when the weekly *New Musical Express* splashed with a full-page front cover photograph of Cyrille Regis in action – ahead of stories about The Who and the Ramones – with the banner headline 'The Human Face of Football'.

When Regis joined Albion from Hayes FC he was offered a one-year deal of £60 per week. Coming from non-league, he was a calculated risk who had to convince the club of his worth. Once he had done so his pay was raised to £200 per week. Cunningham, by contrast, joined the club after five years at Leyton Orient, with a rising reputation, and was offered a longer-term, three-year deal that paid him £120 per week. So there was the odd situation whereby at the end of the 1979 season, one of the most successful in West Brom's history, the star player was the lowest-paid footballer at the club. When he raised the matter with Atkinson he was told to wait until the end of the season before discussing new terms.

'In those days,' Regis explains, 'they offered you a new contract at the end of each season. They never told you. Nobody talked about it beforehand. It was the same for Laurie, they never told him he was playing well or that he'd get more, it was left open. Come the end of the season he's still on £120, I'm on £200 and there was no new contract on offer, so there's a gap there.' With the club allowing the situation to drift, Cunningham began to weigh up his options. He was helped by new employment laws that simplified freedom of movement for employees in member states of the European Economic Community. New freedom of contract legislation meant footballers were no longer tied to their clubs on option clauses; once their contracts had expired they could move freely to another club. By allowing his contract to run down, Cunningham held a stronger bargaining position than would have previously been possible. He asked Albion for £75,000 a year to keep him at the club while at the same time exploring other options by writing to the top European clubs (his girlfriend Nikki typed up the letters) – including Real Madrid, Valencia and Inter Milan – informing them of his availability. Real Madrid already had a file on Cunningham and had been closely monitoring his progress since his electrifying display against Valencia in the UEFA Cup the previous November. So when they received a 'situations wanted' letter from the player they lost no time in contacting Albion chairman Bert Millichip.

Cyrille Regis believes the club's prevarication should and could have been avoided and that Cunningham would have stayed if they had been prepared to talk directly with him. He needed to feel appreciated and, as was shown at Orient, responded best when he felt he was being dealt a straight hand. By being fobbed off he felt undervalued. Regis laments, 'We had a fantastic side that should have been kept together. They let Laurie go and they let Len Cantello go – he had a fantastic partnership in midfield with Bryan Robson. You'd have thought they have got to keep this team together ... It didn't make sense to sell someone young and bring in someone new. Laurie had this chemistry with me and Ally Brown and they let him go. When you buy someone new there is a different chemistry, a different synergy.'

Since joining Albion, Cunningham had taken occasional advice from Ambrose Mendy whom he had known since they played together on the schoolboy football circuits. Mendy is an unusual and interesting man. In his time he has been a boxing promoter, sports agent, nightclub owner and served time in prison for burglary and fraud. He is now a business consultant with well-appointed offices near Bond Street in central London. When Cunningham was an apprentice at Arsenal, Mendy was at Chelsea and he recalls the all-black kick-abouts they played in that were held on Hackney Marshes. 'I don't think anybody thought they were better than Laurie, he was absolutely the prince of all footballers ... in my age nobody made it as black Londoners. He was self-sustained, we all knew he was going to be a superstar.'

With a similar background and mutual interests, including music, Cunningham respected the opinion of the articulate

146

and savvy Mendy. The deal that took him to Madrid was overseen by Bert Millichip and his counterpart at Madrid, Luis de Carlos, at an Italian restaurant in Birmingham. The figure agreed was a staggering £950,000. Shortly afterwards, Mendy travelled with Cunningham to Madrid to discuss personal terms, not as his agent, more as an advisor. Negotiating via an interpreter had its comic element as the pair attempted to increase the numbers in their favour. Mendy recalls the to-ing and fro-ing. 'The interpreter said "money" so Laurie was kicking me under the table; so I figured he was on £300 or £400 a week so I thought let's double it, triple it to £1,200 so he's getting at least £4,000 a month. So we requested a break, and when they returned, finally they said '£5,000 a week, are we close?" ... They meant a week, not a month! We had undervalued it ... you could raise at any time.'

The transfer settled in the early hours of a Thursday morning in a Birmingham trattoria was stunning affirmation of the talent of Laurie Cunningham. His phenomenal season ended in a way that nobody could have foreseen. He was about to join the most famous football club in the world and embarking on the adventure of a lifetime. It seems odd, almost innocent now, how the deal was struck without an entourage of lawyers and agents but face-to-face, and in a matter of days. He telephoned his friend and old Leyton Orient teammate Bobby Fisher the next day to give him the news. Fisher recalls the conversation: "'I'm going to be a millionaire by Saturday. Have a look at the news." And that was it.'

6

EL NEGRITO

One of my favourite photographs of Laurie Cunningham was taken in July 1979, the summer he joined Real Madrid. It shows him heading for the departure gate at Heathrow Airport with the West Bromwich Albion director John Gordon. Although he would return to England to play for Manchester United, Leicester City and Wimbledon for short spells over the next decade, this is the moment he left England as a superstar in waiting. The twenty-three-year-old player seems happy as he glides past the lens; you can sense the anticipation and excitement, the potential of greater things to come. He looks every inch the cosmopolitan European with his silk T-shirt and jacket, with sunglasses stylishly hooked on to the breast pocket: a young man going places. The Spanish press reported that he brought five suitcases of clothes with him when he arrived; he might easily be mistaken for a member of the jet set on his way to the beaches and casinos of the Riviera. Gordon, an avuncular, well-to-do businessman whose family had fled the Nazis in the 1930s to England, was travelling with Cunningham to finalise the transfer and was also a personal friend of the player and his girlfriend Nikki. He enjoyed the couple's sense of mischief, such as the time they travelled together on a plane and pretended not to know who he was for the entire journey. 'He was a bit like our dad,' Nikki fondly recalls. Of course he could not have known what lay ahead for his friend or how his career would play out.

The deal that brought Cunningham to Real Madrid was the biggest in the Spanish club's history. He was the first Englishman to sign for the club and only the second ever black player after the Brazilian Didi's short-lived tenure in 1958, and expectations for the dazzling winger were high. Madrid had endured a long lean spell and not won the European Cup, a competition they had helped form, since 1966 when they dominated Europe with a legendary side that included the all-time greats Alfredo Di Stéfano, Ferenc Puskás and Francisco 'Paco' Gento. He seemed to have hit the jackpot but the mouth-watering fee came with some unwritten terms and conditions. Anybody who represented the club was expected to follow a code of behaviour that extended well beyond mere professionalism on the pitch. A traditional conservative morality pervaded the club and for non-Spaniards like Cunningham and Nikki, unaware of its mores and subtleties, offence could unwittingly be given simply by being themselves. Nikki says, 'Of course we were their nightmare.' Not long after she arrived with her unkempt red hair and quirky way of dressing, a group of players' wives were delegated to take her out shopping: 'They thought that conservative clothes were stylish. They took me to the equivalent of Harrods and picked me out clothes, suggested I cut my hair in a neater way, they spoke to me about my dress sense.' Living together was a problem too for a club which preferred its players to be married and operated a separate pay structure for married and single players.

This patriarchal system had been established by Santiago Bernabéu, the mythical figure after whom the stadium is named. A former player who became president in 1943 and ran the club for almost forty years, he created the modern Real Madrid through land purchases, stadium building, shrewd political partnerships and ruthless commercial expansion – and turned it into a powerhouse of European football, which won the first five European Cups with probably the best team the continent has ever seen. When he died in 1978, 100,000 people filed past his open casket. A tough, cigar-smoking disciplinarian with a flat boxer's nose who was prone to foul-mouthed tirades, he controlled everything at the club. In his book about the aged rivalry between Real Madrid and Barcelona, *Fear and Loathing in La Liga*, the Madrid-based British football writer Sid Lowe writes, 'Bernabéu was to be consulted on everything from ticket prices to players' relationships to match officials. No one dared defy him. On occasions Bernabéu referred to the players as "children". He didn't care much for fashions, either. One Madrid player recalls rushing to the bathroom to shave when Bernabéu turned up at the team hotel. Others remember the president demanding that they cut their hair. Team meals were often held in silence and he refused to let them buy cars and certainly not flash cars: it took two years for Alfredo Di Stefano to get one.'

Hard-headed and right-wing, he had fought on the Nationalist side during the Civil War but later distanced himself from the regime after he encountered difficulties pushing through plans for stadium development. But Bernabéu, who was born in the 1890s, was also an increasingly anachronistic figure. Society had begun to shift after the death of Franco in 1975, ending years of brooding introspection underpinned by rigid Catholic morality in

Spain. The relaxation of censorship and an increase in tourism in the 1960s allowed people greater freedom. In Madrid the capital was beginning to experience a social revolution that became known as La Movida Madrileña ('the Madrileña scene') which reached its height in the mid-1980s. The austere years were replaced with a counter-cultural flourish, clubs and bars stayed open all night and popular culture erupted. A new dynamism energised film, magazines, literature, music and the arts. Madrid became a liberal and exciting destination as long-standing taboos were swept aside. The film-maker Pedro Almodóvar, who rose to prominence during this time with his camp, sexually liberated films, has described the period as 'one of the most explosive moments in the country'. Laurie Cunningham had arrived in a city that was in the mood to party but contracted to a football club whose sober public image seemed firmly rooted in the past.

Rob Hughes marked the transfer in his column for the *International Herald Tribune* by writing an open letter to Antonio Calderon, chief executive of Real Madrid. Hughes, who had followed Cunningham's career since he was a seventeen-year-old at George Petchey's Leyton Orient, counselled Calderon on the player's innocence and vulnerability – which he feared might be misunderstood by the Spanish giants. Alluding to the fact they had not won the European Cup, a competition with which they were obsessed for many years, he stated, 'Madrid's past demands triumph beyond Spain's shores,' and continued, 'you acquire a player capable of raising wing play to an art form ... with the rhythm and movement of dance.' Then the warning:

'Whatever you do, Señor Calderon, don't attempt to impose discipline that cuts out the dance. It has been tried and failed.' Hughes's perspicacity was to prove prophetic a year later when an injured Cunningham was fined one million pesetas after being seen in a high-profile nightclub with his foot in plaster, a disastrous incident that lingered long in the public consciousness – and remains a defining image of his time in Spain even today. Hughes also commented on 'the brutalizing effects of the Spanish tackle which even Johann Cruyff described as potentially crippling,' and concluded that – though at first he might find the player 'non-existent as a conversationalist' – given time he would discover he was 'likeable, sensible and forthcoming ... a dreamer certainly, a player that long ago dreamed himself into another Pelé'.

Cunningham was unveiled before 20,000 excited fans at an open training session at the Bernabéu and proceeded to make an immediate faux pas – and astonish his teammates – when he boldly put the ball through the legs of club captain Camacho. Fellow player Del Bosque quickly pulled him aside and whispered 'Don't ever do that again, son!' while the German Uli Stielike, the other foreign player at the club at the time, later dryly commented, 'nutmegging is part of football. However I can imagine in Camacho's case that Cunningham's next touch of the ball would see a nice, hard tackle coming in.' What may have seemed innocuous and amusing at West Brom was a wholly different matter in Madrid. With no support network to fall back on, Cunningham and Nikki relied on their friendship with John Gordon, who, when he was around, acted as mentor and advisor to them both. He had got to know the couple well when they were near neighbours in Edgbaston in Birmingham. Nikki explains, 'He came on the first few trips to Madrid and visited us often and stayed with us. He had this big comb-over and it would swap sides after he'd had a few drinks, it only took a couple of glasses of wine for him to get rosy-cheeked and he'd get a bit squiffy. He'd question us … we were both dreamers and he was fabulous with us and he went along with it, but he worried how Real Madrid were going to cope with us. We needed managers, and when John Gordon died we were on our own.' Playful behaviour and public demonstrations of affection were frowned upon. Nikki describes a pool party where she fell foul of the rules: 'The party was very sophisticated and the wives never got in the pool and had three changes of costume. I was there in a bikini diving into the pool on top of Laurie's head and he'd lift me up and throw me around. That behaviour was anathema to the high-ups – the Spanish wives didn't behave like that.' Later, she was told she was a distraction and shown press cuttings that described her as a sex symbol; the club banned her from going to the training ground. 'I was really hurt, I was just being myself. After that I didn't go out for a week.'

Cunningham, the first Englishman to play for Real Madrid, followed in the wake of expensive foreign imports to La Liga – Johann Cruyff was the first to join when he signed for Barcelona in 1973 after the ban on foreign players was lifted. He was followed in the same year by Günter Netzer, the glamorous German midfielder, who joined Real Madrid. Netzer might have looked like a playboy with his shoulder-length blond hair and penchant for fast cars, but his speed, strength and astute passing met with considerable success during his three years at the club, Madrid won the title twice, and he later confirmed that they were 'the best organised club in the world ... really they do everything for you.' On the relaxed lifestyle in the capital he remarked, 'at the club you work very hard but outside you find that people have a different mental approach to life. It's not as hectic, not so hectic at all.'

Cunningham made his first appearance in the famous all-white strip in the Santiago Bernabéu Memorial Trophy, a pre-season warm-up tournament against the cream of European teams, Bayern Munich, Ajax and A.C. Milan, in the first weekend of September. Running out for the most illustrious club in Europe in front of the most critical of crowds, was a test of temperament that Cunningham passed with flying colours. Playing against A.C. Milan he scored a penalty and ran the Italian defence ragged all evening, the *Daily Express* noting that 'the Italians by the finish were queuing up to tackle him, his elusiveness occupying three men.' The buoyant mood inside the ground left Cunningham beaming with triumph and relief but when he was asked by a reporter about his availability for an upcoming England international his answer was equivocal: 'It's in my contract that I am released for important games, although in a sense Real still have the last word.' He told reporters at the time of signing that he had a clause in his contract that guaranteed him permission to play for England. This was not the case and throughout his time at Madrid he would find it difficult to obtain release for England matches. Without an agent to review his contract he was exposed, and Madrid repeatedly blocked him from playing for his country, maintaining the right to refuse permission if they had an 'important' game on the weekend after an international fixture.

Cunningham was refused permission to play in two European Championship qualifying games in 1979 and later in 1982 barred from a World Cup warm-up for misconduct. An FA spokesman at the time commented: 'I don't know what Laurie has got in his contract, but it is clearly not as watertight as Kevin Keegan's. Keegan has a guarantee that Hamburg will release him. Cunningham thought he had got the same sort of guarantee when he went to Spain, but he can't have.' When he was picked against Denmark in his first month in Spain, permission was refused and, in a sharp lesson for the player, he was not informed by the club, but found out via a telex sent to the England manager Ron Greenwood with the terse message, 'We regret any inconvenience but, in this instance, the club must come first.' Cunningham was fast learning about Spanish discipline and the downside of Netzer's remark that the club 'do everything for you'.

Cunningham had joined a team that were solid and effective but lacked flair, and it was hoped that his signing would enliven the hard-working team and help them to rediscover the 'connoisseur's football' that had made Real Madrid so famous. Many of the players were graduates from the youth team and the side was known as the 'Madrid of the Garcías' as the squad included keeper García Remón, García Hernández, García Cortés, García Navajas and Pérez García. The leading goalscorer was Carlos Santillana, a fearsome and unparalleled header of the ball who was ably supplied by speedy winger Juanito. Uli Stielike was a tireless presence in midfield beside the young playmaker Vicente Del Bosque (in 2010 the World Cup-winning manager of Spain) and the archetypal hard-tackling defender Gregorio Benito at centre back. It was a team of strong characters under the new management of coach Vujadin Boškov, a Yugoslav who had come from Real Zaragoza.

Boškov was a stickler for training and believed in working his players hard, yet loved the inspiration that Cunningham at his best could bring to the team. In the official team photo taken at the beginning of the season, Cunningham stands out as the only black face among a group of muscly white players, most with long, dark hair in tight-fitting, short-sleeved club shirts. The positioning of the players and staff is significant too. Cunningham, the new signing, squats on his haunches in the front row, standing above him and taking pride of place in the centre of the photograph, is Real Madrid president Luis de Carlos – the successor and protégé of Santiago Bernabéu. Behind him in the third row stands the tracksuited Boškov. The president is flanked on either side by leading players Del Bosque and Stielike, and in that formation you have the power structure of the club: president, senior players and manager.

On 10 September 1979, Laurie Cunningham made his competitive debut for Real Madrid against Valencia at the Bernabéu. To make the occasion even more auspicious Valencia were managed by Real Madrid's most famous son, Alfredo Di Stéfano, the bluff Argentinian who had captained the great 1960s side. Dynamic, charismatic, hard-working and professional, he was the embodiment of the traditional qualities of the club. He did not suffer fools gladly and had little time for flattery. Of the huge transfer fee his old club had paid for the winger he said, 'Cunningham must be the best attacker in the world considering how much Madrid have paid for him.' The new boy scored twice in a 2–1 victory. The press went wild for him and proudly announced he had gone through '*la puerta grande*', or the main gate, a bullfighting metaphor (a matador either exits by the back door in disgrace or leaves carried shoulder high through the main gate). He may even have been hoisted on to the shoulders of fans as the sports newspaper *Marca* joyfully reported his reaction: 'You should have seen the terrified look on the *negrito's* face!'

Cunningham was often referred to as '*El Negrito*' (the little black) or '*El Moreno*' (the brown) in the press and by Madrid fans. The terms may sound reductive, defining a person only by their colour, but it was usually meant without malice. It would be unthinkable for British papers to use such a blunt description (although 'coloured cockney' got a few outings when Cunningham was at Orient). Sid Lowe observes, 'He was viewed by his colour but not to the point of rejection, it was more those horrible clichés – they're good athletes, he's got natural rhythm. There was a kind of fascination ... It was not hateful per se, Spain was at a different phase of immigration to Britain.'

Cunningham seemed to have understood that his nickname was a show of affection: 'they don't mean it in an Alf Garnett way.' He had spent all of his life on the receiving end of overt racial abuse in England yet in Spain it was less vocal, more mannered. There was no monkey chanting at games and no tradition of racism on the terraces, but an illustration of how far the Spanish had yet to come was printed in October 1983, shortly after Cunningham had joined Sporting

Gijón on loan from Madrid. The leading daily paper *ABC*, published in Madrid, splashed on a game in its sports section in which Gijón had beaten league leaders Atlético Madrid 2–0. Praising Cunningham's performance as 'magnificent', and noting Sporting had knocked Atlético off top spot, it described how the player had 'lit a fire as he danced around his opponents.' Unfortunately they chose to illustrate the news with a full-page cartoon on the cover that showed Cunningham smiling, dressed in a loincloth and necklace and holding a spear while dancing around a large bubbling pot in which the Atlético manager Luis Aragónes is cooking over an open fire. The caption reads: 'How Cunningham overcame Atlético.' Even though the piece was complimentary to the player and meant as a joke against Aragónes and Atlético, it is toe-curlingly crude.

In November 1979 James Lawton profiled Cunningham in *Soccer Monthly* magazine in an article looking at the impact he was having on a generation of black youths. 'Cunningham has proved beyond doubt that the prejudices which lurked in the minds of so many British football coaches and managers can be assigned to history. Cunningham has done more than fight his way to Real Madrid. He has liberated a whole generation of young blacks.' Referring to a conversation he had with Cunningham two years earlier (when he was at WBA) it is clear that the player had had problems in his career and that the confusion of his early years led him to question himself and his identity as a young black man in Britain. But then things began to change. In one of his most candid and lucid statements he said, 'There have been times when I've been mixed up about the race thing. A couple of years ago I thought that to be a black in England was to be a loser. You know, back of the queue for decent jobs. Suspicion on you before anyone knew what you were about, what you were like inside your skin. I did have a feeling for "Black Power". It seemed to meet the mood of frustration. It could give you some pride. Then I changed. It sort of struck me that the great majority of people, black and white, are in the same boat, fighting for a decent living. It also struck me that down at Orient I was getting a very good break. People were more interested in the fact that I could play a bit than that the colour of my skin was black. Now along comes a guy like Johnny Giles, who knows so much about the game, and lays out all that money for me. I want to tell a lot of those black kids out there the same kind of thing can happen to them.'

He was conscious that he was a role model but shied away from being a figurehead for a cause. He was not a leader in that sense, it was not in his nature. By the words he uses you can see that he is growing as a person. By daring to have the ambition to play for Real Madrid, Cunningham had, as Lawton says, 'more than most, just obliterated the habit of referring to black English footballers.' It's an important point that by playing for Real Madrid Cunningham had raised the profile of black players to such heights that they no longer needed to be defined as 'black', but just as footballers.

In Spanish football the emphasis was on technique and ball control. Ever since he was a boy Cunningham had played thoughtful football. His friends were therefore not surprised when Real Madrid took an interest; they saw him as a maverick in an orthodox world in England, one who would never be fully trusted by most managers. The brief time spent on fitness and conditioning in the First Division was in stark contrast to what took place at Chamartín, Real Madrid's training ground, each day. Ever since his teenage days with Highgate North Hill, Cunningham had been the fittest, strongest player in his team. At Orient he impressed with his perpetual energy and effortlessly dominated both cross-country runs and sprints. At Madrid, where Cunningham and Stielike were the finest athletes, the training routine was relentless and intense. In an interview for the *Observer* in 1980, six months after his debut, Cunningham gave an insight into his new environment. 'This Boškov is special ... The first thing that shook me was after a game in Seville. We came back on the overnight train, got into Madrid about eight and were out training by ten. I couldn't believe it. Now that is a regular thing as far as I am concerned. At West Brom we used to get in at 10, start training about 10.30 and finish about 12. Here you start at 10.30, and that means you have to be changed and ready to go. Boškov takes us out and works us over, then we do technical stuff. There's more variety to it than in England. After lunch we start again and go on till it gets dark. It's hard but I love it.' And inevitably, of course, for a club obsessed with discipline, lateness was penalised with a 1,000 peseta fine (around £10) for every minute a player was late.

On the field Cunningham's star profile made him a target for players keen to introduce him to the dark arts of Spanish defending. After his dream start he suffered torn ligaments and a chipped bone in his second game and was out for three weeks. Injury and long recovery times were characteristic of his career in Spain – and he complained that the medical treatment he received was unsatisfactory and harmful to his career. Cyrille Regis laments, 'He never got through his injuries as he should have done.' Faced with rugged man-to-man marking for the first time he said, 'I seemed to get kicked every second. When I got the ball and turned ... bump, I was on the ground.' And playing wide on the wing where he could quickly fade from a game, Cunningham soon faced criticism in the press. Some asked if Madrid had paid a million pounds for a man to merely take corners with the outside of his foot. Consistency was a problem for the mercurial player who was minutely scrutinised as never before – with every unproductive run or poorly executed pass duly noted.

Although he insisted in interviews that the club were looking after him and that playing for Madrid was a dream come true, he must have often felt alone. Joining a club with some big egos and a core of players who had come through the youth system together, Cunningham was an outsider who did not speak the language. An outsider with an enviable bank balance, too, and it didn't take long for Santillana and Del Bosque to ask for pay rises. Cyrille Regis offers an insight: 'Loneliness is sometimes part of the job. You don't know the language, you've got to build up trust with other people. The first black guy in Madrid, I would think there were times when it would be lonely.' He believes in hindsight that Cunningham was unprepared for life in Spain and too young to deal with all that playing for a club like Real Madrid entailed. 'He wasn't mature enough at twenty-three ... it would have been better if he was twenty-five or twenty-six, he'd only been playing in the top flight for two and a half years. You're not stable, you're still young and the weakest part of a player at that age is their mental strength. Your head. Your emotions. When your body is strong your emotions are weak. Criticisms hurt you, dealing with pressures ... you've got to cope with all that.'

Sections of the Spanish press were never going to be happy whatever he did and were waiting for him to fail, suspecting he was not worth the price tag. One editorial in particular from early 1980 did not pull its punches: 'In a team that is pure fight, where no ball is given up as lost, his posture does not fit. He does not kill, he does not leave his skin on the turf, he does not sweat his shirt ... there are long periods of the game where he is simply not involved at all. It's a lot of money just to take corners with the outside of your foot. If I was a friend of his, I would say: "Laurie, my son, play the whole game, take part. Don't wait, seek. Don't hide, find space. Here you'll get hacked; defenders are like that. Either take risks or go back to the fog of London. It's sunny here and things are seen very clearly."' Cunningham divided opinion and, for all the naysayers, there were plenty who saw a unique talent in the player. In his first season Real Madrid won the League and Cup Double and despite injury problems Cunningham scored twelve goals. His contribution was sporadic but at times extraordinary.

Boškov's assessment of his player is worth noting: 'Laurie is English – you mustn't forget that. It's difficult for an English player to arrive in Spain and be a superstar overnight. But he had a good campaign. He had good games and bad games ... but that's understandable. I think he must participate more. He's too quiet. He doesn't shout. He must tell the others that he wants the ball.' Di Stéfano noted, 'Here the game is very different [from England] with tough man-to-man marking. Next season will be the real test ... now he's got to produce the goods.' Mario Kempes, whose team Valencia had been on the receiving end of Cunningham's wonderful display for West Brom and played against him twice in La Liga, called him ' ... a phenomenon. His ball skills are incredible. And his ball control at top speed is perhaps as good as anybody I've seen.' While Barcelona manager Helenio Herrera an old-school, defensive tough guy, took the opposite, and decidedly partisan view, when he bluntly stated: 'I wouldn't want him in my team. He may be all right for Real Madrid, but I would never be interested in buying him.' The Madrid daily *Diario AS* published a piece in praise of Cunningham and argued he was more sinned against than sinner: 'The big problem that he had last season was that the rest of the team didn't understand him. And even though the Real players deny this in public, there was a fair amount of resentment in the dressing rooms about him earning more money than the others. Next season he needs to develop a greater understanding with his teammates to become a really top star.'

Boškov favoured a 4–3–3 system that built its attack around Cunningham on the left, Juanito on the right and Santillana in the middle as striker. Santillana, the team's top scorer, acknowledged that Cunningham was the only player who could jump higher than him, yet he rarely got the chance to show it as he was charged with taking corners. His inswinging corners, struck with the outside of the foot, looked great on television and became a crowd-pleasing trademark of his game – but they were ultimately counter-productive. It was easier for Santillana to run on to and attack an outswinging corner than it was an inswinger, and by having him take corners Madrid were depriving themselves of Cunningham's presence in the box as he stood marooned by the corner flag. This may partly account for his relatively low goal tally. He complained to Boškov about being isolated on the wing and told him he craved a more free-ranging role in the team. He also came to believe that he was not being given the ball enough by teammates. In midfield Stielike had a natural tendency to direct most of his passes to the right, further isolating Cunningham, yet he is complimentary about the Englishman. 'He was the most complete player I have ever played with: unbelievably quick, both footed, with great timing in the air. His big handicaps were being injury-prone and his private life.'

On 10 February 1980, Real Madrid travelled to the Camp Nou to play Barcelona. '*El Clásico*', as it has become known, is the biggest match of the season for both teams. The history of the fixture is filled with decades of drama, conspiracy theories, acts of genius and betrayal, goals and fouls. It symbolises the antagonism and rivalry between the two greatest football clubs in Spain, perhaps in the world. Any victory is special, an away win even more so. Earlier in the season at the Bernabéu, Madrid had beaten Barcelona 3–2 with Cunningham scoring. For the return fixture at the Camp Nou in front of 100,000 fans, and with millions more watching on television, Cunningham put on an even greater show. His performance that night was probably his best in a Madrid shirt and his dominance, constant changes of speed and mastery of the ball helped Madrid to a 2–0 victory that gave them a vital boost in their title race with Real Sociedad. It also meant they did the double over their nemesis. Playing on the left wing against the Argentinian full back Rafa Zuviría, Cunningham took his opposite number to the cleaners. Zuviría later was honest enough to say, 'That night I had to mark Cunningham but there was no way I could stop him. Everything he did came off for him ... I can say that it was the only night of my life that I couldn't sleep after a game.' Real Madrid substitute Miguel Ángel Portugal had a ringside seat on the bench as the spectacle unfurled before his eyes and couldn't contain his delight when he called out, 'Hey, Rafa! We'll get you a photo of him if you like! Maybe then you'll see what his face looks like! Maybe at the end of the game he'll let you get near enough to shake his hand!' The Barcelona daily *El Mundo Deportivo* ran the headline 'Everything Turned Black for Barcelona' above a picture of Cunningham swerving between two Barça players and described him as 'brilliant' and 'spectacular'. *AS* ran the headline 'Big Bomb in the Camp Nou', and *Marca* reported on the 'black man who plays football like the angels and is called Cunningham', who had 'put the Camp Nou in his pocket'. But more extraordinary than the press reaction was the response of the home supporters, the Barcelona fans, who began to applaud him: 'Each time Cunningham got the ball the ovation was huge', *Marca* enthused. It was unheard of for the Catalan fans to show such approval for a player representing their most hated rivals. Poor Rafa Zuviría, who had yet to endure that sleepless night said, 'I think the applause from the public had a double objective, on the one hand to recognise the merit of our rival and on the other hand to protest at the way we played.' Cunningham's own response was straightforward and to the point, 'What fans! To play in this stadium is a pleasure.'

By April 1980 Madrid had reached the semi-final of the European Cup and been drawn against Kevin Keegan's FC Hamburg. Keegan, who had played with Cunningham in the England team, was, like many, unconvinced by Cunningham and said before the second leg of the tie, 'He's not the sort of player who can dominate for ninety minutes – I've played with him about six times now and I'm still trying to work out his style of play.' Over the two legs Hamburg won 5–3 on aggregate and in the second match played at Hamburg's Volkspark in front of 65,000, Cunningham turned on the style. Patrick Barclay wrote in the *Guardian*: 'Upstaging Kevin Keegan is far from easy, but Cunningham brought it off ... his performance contained pace, skill, courage and above all, the element of individualism that has often been cited as a weakness in his game.' He scored one and hit the crossbar with a fierce drive, but once again Madrid had failed to reach the final of the European Cup. Winning the double at home did not ease the pressure. They had been expected to challenge for and mostly win domestic honours, but what really mattered, and defined them as a club, was victory in Europe and ultimately re-establishing themselves as the premier team on the Continent.

After first living in a hotel then a rented apartment, in September 1980 Cunningham and Nikki moved to a spectacular £200,000 hacienda in the hills outside Madrid. The house in the exclusive Las Matas area – described as the Beverly Hills of Spain, whose former residents included film directors and bullfighters – had panoramic views over the surrounding countryside and the snow-capped Guadarrama Mountains. Franco's former house was visible from one of its terraces. Built in a modernist style and painted white, it sprawled over six levels with a central spiral staircase and boasted six bedrooms and three bathrooms, a huge living area and kitchen, and a swimming pool and tennis court. Set in its own landscaped grounds there was plenty of room for the couple's five dogs, including a Great Dane. Impressive as it looked from behind its iron gates the house was in reality jerry-built and became a costly millstone.

A glorified concrete and glass shell – built on land with poor drainage that flooded whenever it rained, with a partly finished interior of unmade walls and pipes that regularly leaked – the property was sold to him by Gregorio 'Goyo' Benito, his Real Madrid teammate and something of a self-styled entrepreneur. He and Cunningham had become close friends. Benito, another to have come up through the youth ranks, was one of the stronger characters at the club. A hard-tackling defender, he was popular with fellow players who often met at his bar in town to drink and play cards. He revelled in a hardman reputation on the pitch; former players described him admiringly as 'an evil son of a bitch'. In a curious arrangement Cunningham had his mortgage repayments deducted directly from his wages at Real Madrid and paid into Benito's account, a set-up that later led to Cunningham feeling that money was still owed him. Typical of his trusting, at times credulous, nature, Cunningham had bought a superficially beautiful house from a friend he relied upon without taking proper advice.

When it came to business matters such as sponsorship deals he seemed to have little interest in the finer detail and left negotiations to Nikki. She recalls: 'I had to learn Spanish really quickly. I was the only person he trusted. We'd discuss it and decide how we were going to go about it.' Visitors to the house were surprised at what they found. Bobby Fisher, his old Orient teammate, remembers visiting and finding the swimming pool filled with rubble after Cunningham had knocked a wall through but failed to clear away the mess. He found the place sparsely furnished with piles of clothing scattered about, and was generally surprised at the state of it. Nikki, who has warmer memories of the place, claims it was put to good use as a dance studio. 'We had a big house but we'd sleep on the roof looking at the sky ... we had parquet floors so we could tap on it. We had tap shoes and we'd do a rhythm, a call and answer – you'd make up a rhythm and say "find it", you'd go through it for an hour, and we had large mirrors so we could see what we were doing.'

Living outside the city, alone with their dogs, brought the couple closer together. 'When that happens you bond with someone in a completely different way,' Nikki says. 'He never quite got his brilliance, you could never tell him because he just wouldn't have it. He painted a whole wall as a Valentine's card for me once. We had friends' paintings on the wall from their O levels or degrees, not big, expensive pictures. It didn't mean anything really, it had to have relevance for him. They [the club] didn't get it, they thought it was too quirky.' The stability of the relationship was strong but in Catholic Madrid there would always be the question of marriage to be addressed. Nikki remarked in a newspaper that 'there is no open hostility but I do sense they strongly disapprove,' and Cunningham added, 'We're happy as we are and we've no intention of being forced into marriage. We both believe our relationship is more secure than many marriages.' For the couple happy to be left alone to stare at the night sky and dance in their hilltop eyrie, conforming to the expectations of the club hierarchy was a betrayal of their personalities. 'Because of our bond and playfulness we were treated a bit like children,' Nikki says. 'We'd go to Flamenco bars, we loved the darkness of it, the smell of Spanish cigarettes and brandy at 2 a.m. to watch the dancers, we'd absorb it and love it.'

By the end of the season Madrid were league champions and Cunningham had scored twelve goals, eight in the league, three in the European Cup and one in the Copa del Rey. In the final of the Copa, Madrid were up against their own reserve team, Castilla, who played in the Second Division and had been the sensation of the season by beating four top division teams en route to the final. Real won to complete the double but Cunningham did not play well, showing only briefly the skill he was capable of, and left the field to whistles from some fans. He summed up the season as 'not bad for the first season, though the injuries didn't help and it was often difficult for me to play flat out.' It had been a successful season for Madrid but their star signing still had plenty to prove if he wanted to win the fans over completely. But before this could happen bad luck intervened when a cynical foul causing terrible injury all but ruined his career at Madrid.

In November 1980 Real Madrid travelled to Real Betis in Seville. Real were fourth in the table and Cunningham had begun the new campaign well, scoring five goals. Ten minutes into the game, in an off-the-ball incident, he was viciously stamped on by Betis defender Francisco Bizcocho – a foul that went unseen and unpunished. The swingeing assault on his left foot broke his big toe. A victim of vicious defending – the Barcelona captain Asensi had warned, 'Spanish defenders are much more violent and aggressive than in England' – Cunningham would ultimately miss the rest of the season. With arch-rivals Barcelona next up, the Bernabéu press department were keen to downplay the injury. Among the medics opinion differed about the severity of the damage: some thought it was not much more than bruising, others felt it was more serious, but he was not sent to hospital for an X-ray. Cunningham returned for '*El Clásico*' and played the full ninety minutes, presumably in some pain, but was a shadow of the player who had earned the adulation of Barça aficionados nine months earlier.

After further checks the senior club doctor Lopez Quiles told the press: 'The club thought there was nothing wrong with him but he had an injury that needed treating. They ended up calling me after the second match. I had to operate.' Told to go home and rest, Cunningham made the worst possible decision when he went out forty-eight hours later, with his foot in plaster, to Pacha, a nightclub in the centre of Madrid, with Nikki and some friends. Both press and club came down hard on him. From then on his image as a disco-loving dilettante who didn't care enough about his talent or fitness was set in stone. Seen 'dancing' with his foot in plaster, Cunningham claimed it was a case of mistaken identity, that it was in fact a black friend of his, but the fallout was dramatic. One teammate insists, 'This was the moment that destroyed him because of the reputation it lumbered him with but also, and much more importantly, because it was confirmation of an injury, of the start of a series of injuries, that ruined a wonderful player.'

The club were swift to respond and a spokesman announced, 'It is the first time in eighty years that one of our players has defied doctor's orders. He didn't have authorisation to go out and he neglected his physical integrity ... He needs discipline.' He was fined a club record million pesetas, the stiffest ever in Spanish football. As the story broke, a shocked Cunningham was besieged in the Las Matas house by reporters and TV crews where teammate Goyo Benito stood at the gates assuring the gathered throng that his friend was contrite after he had 'torn him to strips'. A humbled Cunningham gave his version of events in an interview: 'The doctor saw me in the morning and told me that I was OK and gave me permission to go home and he asked me to pass by the clinic on Monday for another test. In the evening some friends came by and wanted to go out. I believed I was free until Monday and it wouldn't matter if I went to bed late because I could not play for a month and a half, so I said yes ... I only went once to the toilet and when I came back I moved a little bit to the music, but look I've got a plaster cast on, no one can dance with this on. I stayed in the disco until 3.30 a.m. even though the club tells the players that they must be in bed by 11 p.m. but I understood that I was free until Monday. I know it was wrong but that's what I believed. On Monday morning I spoke to director Fernández Trigo. He told me that I was not to join with the squad until all of this was cleared up.'

The incident gave fans the opportunity to vent their frustration on Cunningham. Perhaps if he had been more consistent in games he might have been given a fairer hearing but a *Marca* journalist wrote what many fans were thinking: 'Sixteen months after he cost Madrid $2 million he still has not shown he is worth the money – and now he's gone and got injured. Real Madrid are hopping mad and with all the justification in the world.' What should have only taken a couple of months to heal ended up taking the rest of the season and he needed a second operation. The first operation on his toe by Lopez Quiles was not successful and after advice from fellow players he sought a second opinion from a specialist doctor in Barcelona named Villadot. Lopez Quiles maintained he had not made an error: 'It's not my fault what happened there. The intervention that I made resulted in my opinion in a satisfactory outcome. What happened afterwards is that he had subsequent problems and medically it was considered that he had to go through surgery again so these complications did not recur. An expert in this field is Dr Villadot.' Cunningham also consulted a Harley Street specialist who told him bluntly that his toe would never heal properly. In an attempt at damage limitation Cunningham was forced into making a written apology to Luis de Carlos to try and salvage his place at the club. He wrote contritely, and rather formally, probably after taking advice, of his sadness at putting the club in such a position and of his pride in playing for Real Madrid and added: 'I am very sorry that my performances up until now have not been as hoped ... I am waiting impatiently for the day I can return to my teammates to advance the honour and glory of the club.'

Sidelined and with a sullied reputation, Cunningham's career was starting to unravel. Real Madrid, who had never trusted his lifestyle or his marital status, were left with a costly invalid on the books with whom they were fast losing patience; while Cunningham could justifiably feel that he had not been well looked after by the club. Most worryingly the toe injury directly affected his game: his lightning burst of pace was fatally compromised and his game would never be the same again.

7

'BAD LUCK ... LIKE WITCHCRAFT'

Taking refuge in his hillside mansion – what one publication had called 'Laurie's castle' – Cunningham was entering an introspective phase of his career. He was now more cautious and less trusting than before. Before coming to Spain he had always been open and approachable – and one reason for retreating to the hills of Las Matas was to escape the legions of autograph hunters and hangers-on he encountered whenever he walked the streets of Madrid. Nikki said at the time: 'The fans have been marvellous but their attitude to footballers can be a bit off-putting. They'll stand around him only a couple of feet away and just gape silently. If we walk in the street, cars will suddenly start swerving towards us so that the drivers can get a closer look.'

The bruising response to his 'indiscreet Saturday night fever', as one tabloid put it, forced him to examine his position at Real Madrid for the first time. Stung by the draconian measures the club had taken, and increasingly aggrieved by his medical care (he had to undergo a second operation on his toe in March 1981 – when the cast was removed a problem was found with the cartilage and he was told he would be out for another six weeks), he withdrew further into himself. Old friends detected a change. Bobby Fisher recalled a visit to Spain where he noticed 'his whole philosophy of life had changed, he wasn't Mr Free and Easy. You could see he had changed. What looked like a dream turned into a nightmare. I never saw him smile once.' And Cyrille Regis remembered the state of the house: 'It was always left half-done, "I'll get round to it later."' His sharply dressed friend did not even own a washing machine.

A depressing routine of doctors' appointments, rehab sessions and sitting around at home, started to establish itself. Unable to train and deprived of the camaraderie of the dressing room, he must have felt a peripheral figure. Brooding at home put a strain on his relationship with Nikki too, and left to their own devices the pair struggled to deal with the fallout. Nikki says wistfully, 'A lot of the time we didn't know what to do,' and it began to take its toll on the way they behaved. 'I wasn't happy. We were becoming snobs,' she says. The moment it struck hardest was when they went out for dinner with a group of players one evening and at the end of the meal 'they left the waiter one peseta each and he had worked his feet off serving them. They could have left 100 pesetas each, it would have meant nothing to them ... we were treating him like he was the underclass. There was a snobbishness around and people were showing off their wealth.'

It was the start of the era of the celebrity footballer, where there was a chance to make a lot of money beyond the game for the shrewd and business aware, perhaps best personified by Kevin Keegan. He had formed his own company as early as 1972 and by the time Cunningham was in Spain had released a top forty hit single, advertised aftershave on television, endorsed board games and playing cards and sold tens of thousands of plastic footballs with his name on. Cunningham's observations are interesting: 'I could never be commercialised like Kevin Keegan. I am not into that and I don't want to be.' Although it may have gone against his best intentions, living the life of a remote and wealthy footballer in a large, gated house, it was difficult to remain unaffected by circumstances. And as the injury dragged on into springtime the bad press kept coming: 'The worst thing isn't that Cunningham goes to a disco and dances more than a Zulu. It's February and there's still no chance of him being back. It's only a toe; lucky it's not a leg,' one contributor whined.

On the pitch, after an inconsistent few months, Madrid were in a position to challenge for honours by the end of the 1980–1981 season. As the final day of the season approached they were level on points with Basque side Real Sociedad and the race for the title went down to the wire in a dramatic finale – worthy of the unlikely prisoner-of-war football film *Escape to Victory*, which came out that year – with Real Sociedad snatching the title from Madrid's grasp after scoring a goal in the last fifteen seconds of their match against Sporting Gijón to deny them glory. As news filtered through to the Madrid players their premature celebrations turned to despair. One player, Juanito, was so distraught that he walked off the pitch on his knees. The shattering end to the season was hard to take but Real had a bigger prize to look forward to. Despite their injury-hit year the team made good progress in Europe and after beating Inter Milan in the semi-finals had reached the European Cup Final – giving themselves an opportunity to finally emerge from the shadow of the fabled 1960s side. They were to play Liverpool in Paris, the city where they had won their first ever European title, and Boškov made his intentions on selection clear when he told reporters, 'I am counting on Cunningham in Paris: he has eleven days to reach peak fitness.' After a fifteen-year absence Real were back in the final of the competition that defined them. It was an impressive achievement for a team that hadn't really expected to get that far and even the most committed fans must have doubted if they were good enough to beat Liverpool, a team which had won the competition twice in four years.

After six months out of action it was a tall order to expect Cunningham to play for ninety minutes but Boškov must have hoped he would come good for long enough to cause some damage. He set his team up defensively, identifying Graeme Souness as Liverpool's main threat. If he could be stopped from controlling midfield, he reasoned, Madrid's greater individual skill could dominate the game. To this effect he brought Camacho forward from defence to negate Souness with the intention of marking him out of the game. Juanito, the skilful winger, and perhaps the most gifted player of all, was also moved to midfield to orchestrate the attack.

As the final drew closer pressure was applied from above: Cunningham received a phone call from one of the directors enquiring about his fitness and seeking assurances about his commitment to the club. He then told him plainly he must play in the final or else his career at the club was over. The game was played at the Parc des Princes in front of 48,300 fans on an uneven lumpy pitch that made passing difficult and it soon settled into a dull, attritional midfield contest.

The cagey opening minutes never developed into anything more exciting and the match, played at walking pace at times, descended into a boring and scrappy affair. Playing on the left Cunningham seemed to be running with the brakes on; there was no evidence of his devastating pace and he looked tentative and uncertain. Early on in the first half he was put through with a deft pass from Santillana but, instead of running the ball to the touchline, he eased up and cut inside before fruitlessly giving it away. The poor condition of the pitch – which had seen a rugby match played on it the day before – caused awkward unpredictable bounces and led to some comical-looking efforts on goal from the likes of Kenny Dalglish, Terry McDermott and Juanito. Shots from either team were rare, as Liverpool played a cautious, defensive game. One French newspaper summed it up as 'chloroform football'. It was one of the ironies of the match that Cunningham, who was best-equipped to run at defenders and open up the game, was hamstrung by injury and patently could not do so. He played a passive, peripheral role and although he switched sides often and played on the left and right wings, he posed little threat and spent too much of the game isolated and ineffective.

As the game progressed hopeful fifty-yard punts at goal from midfield only added to the agony of it all. It is telling that Graeme Souness, Liverpool's designated danger man, did not have a shot at goal until the last five minutes. Madrid's best chance came early in the second half and fell to Camacho, the defender moved up to cope with Souness, who unexpectedly found himself one-on-one with Liverpool goalkeeper Ray Clemence, but proceeded to float the ball tamely over the bar. Appropriately, it was a defender who scored the winning goal. After eighty-one minutes, Alan Kennedy ran on to a throw-in and chested the ball past a floundering García Cortés, before charging into the Madrid penalty area and neatly slotting home. Shortly afterwards an encouraging move saw Cunningham run on to a pass and into a good attacking position but he slipped, forcing him to pass the ball sideways and with all momentum lost the attack broke down. In one of the dullest finals for years Liverpool celebrated a 1–0 victory, their third success in the competition, adding to their wins in Rome in 1977 and London in 1978.

Cunningham would never be the same again. The months he had spent in recuperation had been ruinous. During its time in plaster the injured toe became rigid and lost all flexibility and his graceful, gliding running style, upright and on the balls of his feet, was compromised for good. It is surprising that Boškov kept him on for the whole game as he must have known he was not fully fit. He played the match in pain and diminished, wastefully hitting stray passes and making poor crosses the longer it went on.

Madrid lost patience. On their biggest night for years their most expensive player had been found wanting. They finished the season without any silverware, being knocked out of the Copa del Rey shortly afterwards, and would not win the league again for a further six years. Perhaps it was the after-effects of coming so close to winning the league and then playing so poorly in the European Cup Final within the space of one disastrous month. For Boškov and Cunningham the writing was on the wall as scapegoats were sought by detractors within the club. Cunningham would only play a handful more games in a Real Madrid shirt after that fateful night in Paris.

When the new season got under way there was no starting place for Cunningham in the first team and he tried to work his way back in to Boškov's consideration. Then, in September, as the team were preparing for the start of their UEFA Cup campaign, bad luck once again intervened in Cunningham's career. In a routine training session he was fiercely tackled by defender Pérez García and left writhing in pain. Unable to carry on, he hobbled back to the dressing room. Interviewed in his hospital bed the next day with a heavily strapped left leg, he said, 'I believe that I have got bad luck with me like witchcraft, yeah luck is definitely not on my side ... I still don't know what's wrong with me. I think it might be minor ligament damage but I won't know until tomorrow when I receive the results of the scan.' His fears were well-founded, the scans showing he had indeed ruptured ligaments in his knee. Cynics may have suspected foul play from a jealous teammate, but Uli Stielike sees it differently: 'It must have been an accident as Pérez García was as fair a sportsman as you would wish to meet.' Yet again Cunningham was laid up. At the age of twenty-five he should have been reaching his prime as a player not spending days, weeks, on the treatment benches. An operation was performed but took six months to heal, all but ending his season; and he later claimed he was misdiagnosed and that a damaged meniscus (a fibrous cartilage in the knee) was the real cause of his injury, not the ligaments. Bad luck and bad press had conspired to shred his reputation as one of the brightest young players in Europe as he battled to save his career at a club which, only two years earlier, had greeted his arrival with such fanfare.

Nikki noticed a change in her boyfriend around this time: 'When he realised he was a star it started to go wrong for him because that arrogance wasn't in him.' She had changed too and found herself becoming blasé about money and possessions. She bemoans the superficial glamour of their life together as soulless and empty: 'When you are living that life you are in a goldfish bowl and it changes where you can go and who you can trust. What do people want from you? Are they racist? Do you want me for access to something, are you genuine? The more money we made the less we paid for stuff.' Everything was provided or readily available: 'We got first-class flights with Iberia because we knew most of the captains, we could go straight to the cabin crew lounge and get flights and they knew in return they would have the best seats at the next Real Madrid home game. Cars were given to you, stereos, clothes, furniture all sorts of stuff … [when that happens] you lose the drive, that slight edge you had. We had a real silk sofa – why do we need a £20,000 sofa? Think again! We could get a nice sofa for a tenth of that.' Feeling a fraud and traduced by the endless press interest in her relationship, self-doubt and self-loathing turned into unhappiness, and the couple grew apart. Nikki believed Cunningham had achieved everything he had set out to do and could return to England with his head held high. She asked him to leave with her, hoping he would say yes or that he could be released, but deep down knew he couldn't. He was contracted to the club for a further three years. Feeling that she could no longer go on as things were she left and returned to England early in 1982.

Cunningham must have wondered what else could go wrong for him. Unsettled in his personal life and struggling to get fit and play regular football again, the World Cup, to be held in Spain later that summer, was fast approaching. As his fitness gradually returned Boškov gave him a run out in the league and then included him in the starting line-up for a UEFA Cup tie against German side FC Kaiserslautern in March. If he could reclaim his past form perhaps he could get himself back into contention for a place in the England World Cup squad. In the first leg played at the Bernabéu he scored an early goal and with confidence flowing through the side Real won the match easily 3–1, putting themselves in a strong position for the return fixture. However the second leg could not have gone worse as Madrid suffered a humiliating 5–0 thrashing, and to add insult to injury had three men sent off. First to see red was Cunningham himself, who kicked out pointlessly and petulantly at an opponent for no reason as he was running away from him right in front of the referee. It looked like the act of a man who knew his days at the club were numbered. Such lack of discipline infuriated Luis de Carlos and for it to happen so publicly was viewed as an act of gross insubordination. As punishment, as well as being fined by the club, he was barred from playing in an England World Cup warm-up match later that month in Bilbao. With the sending off, Cunningham – either consciously or not – put his career as a first-team player on the line that night. It was an impetuous act that was totally out of character.

A week later Boškov was dismissed. Luis Molowny, a former Madrid manager, was brought in as interim coach until the end of the season. He steered them to the Copa del Rey Final and they beat Sporting Gijón 2–1 to win the trophy to complete what was by their standards a mediocre season. Cunningham played the whole game but not well. *ABC* gave him a zero rating, the only player in the match to receive this dubious honour. Nevertheless he had picked up his third winner's medal with Real Madrid.

Left out of the England World Cup squad, and with the tournament taking place on his doorstep (and the final due to be played at the Bernabéu), Cunningham must have felt bitterly frustrated at what might have been. One of the reasons he had signed in 1979 was to gain valuable experience of Spain to better place himself in the mind of England manager Ron Greenwood, for a call-up to the squad. Any self-pity was partly eased by an extended visit from his brother Keith who came to stay with him at Las Matas for the duration of the tournament. By this time Cunningham had become friendly with John Fitzgibbon, an Irishman who ran the Sportsman Bar in central Madrid. Commonplace these days, it was the first of its kind in the capital. Cunningham grew to trust Fitzgibbon, who later acted as an advisor and was best man at his wedding in 1986. He remembers Cunningham at this time as being 'a bit down about his career but he wanted to make the most of it. His Spanish was good and he loved the way of life.' He would usually go to the bar for lunch with one or two teammates and outwardly seemed content: 'He was fun to be with, he always had a smile, he was a good person.' During the World

Cup Fitzgibbon organised a parallel five-a-side tournament – where England took on France, Italy and Spain – in which Keith took part, with his younger brother acting as manager to the England side for one fixture.

Adjusting to disappointment in his career had become part of Cunningham's life in Spain, but nothing could prepare him for the tragedy that befell his family in London later that summer. Keith had recently set up home with his girlfriend Norma Richards and her three daughters in a flat in Dalston, east London. While he was away in Spain he received the shocking news that Norma and two of her daughters, Samantha, aged nine, and Syretta, seven, had been murdered in the family home. The Cunningham brothers immediately left for London (Laurie was given compassionate leave by Real Madrid) to grieve with their family and spend fruitless hours asking in clubs and bars if anybody could help with information about the killings. The crime remained unsolved for over twenty-five years, until the football writer Peter Law contacted Scotland Yard about it in 2008, and a cold case review was generated, which led to the conviction of a local man called Wilbert Anthony Dyce in 2010.

The time spent organising the funeral arrangements and supporting his grief-stricken family meant that Cunningham missed the start of the season. Madrid president Luis de Carlos appeared to be supportive: 'We are offering every type of help,' he said. 'This boy is a fantastic person, but he has no luck, but he must know that the club is at his side with anything he may need in these difficult moments.' The sympathy was no doubt genuine and well-intentioned, as was the period of leave granted to the player. However, over the summer Madrid had announced a new appointment, when their most famous and illustrious former player Alfredo Di Stéfano took over as manager. The only other person to be held in the same regard as Santiago Bernabéu by Madrid fans, he had made Bernabéu's dreams flesh and in doing so brought undying fame and glory to the club.

Another change saw the arrival of Dutch international Johnny Metgod from AZ Alkmaar. This was a troubling development for Cunningham: league rules allowed only two foreigners to play in any team and with Uli Stielike a mainstay of the side, his future in the first team looked uncertain. As far as Di Stéfano was concerned Cunningham was a fringe player and he preferred to play Metgod. The unsentimental manager demanded blood, sweat and tears from his players and had little time for anybody who didn't conform to his unshakeable view of the game. With two years left to run on his contract Cunningham was in limbo. Instructed to register for Castilla, Madrid's reserve team, he refused and so a stalemate developed between club and player. Still the highest-paid player at the club, the prospect of another team taking him on loan and paying his wages was slim, especially with his track record of injuries. Sitting around waiting to play did him no good and, as resentment built in him, he went public with criticisms of the club. In an interview with *El País* in September 1982 to mark the second anniversary of the foot stamp that had broken his toe, headlined 'The Doctors at Real Madrid have taken two years out of my career', he vented his anger. The futility of his situation prompted him to act to try and salvage his career and to give a riposte to the bad publicity he had been enduring for so long.

In the interview he states, 'I still don't understand how I can be operated on twice on my left big toe and twice on my knee. Even the best medical experts have told me that I've made a mistake. I've had a lot of time to reflect and this is not normal. They opened my knee to fix the ligament and still didn't understand that my meniscus was also bad. It's been a terrible time, incredible; I wouldn't wish it on any sportsperson.' He continues, 'Before all this I was really looking forward to the World Cup to be able to show myself off internationally and now it's only a dream. I don't dream any more about World Cups, I only dream of being able to play football again.' Then, in an echo of his 'situations wanted' approach to Real Madrid three years earlier, he adds, 'It's evident in Madrid I have no future ... that's why I would like the club to release me on loan to an English team for the rest of the season, that way I can at least get some games and recover some rhythm that I've lost over the past two years. The problem is at this moment there are very few teams who would pay my contract for a definitive transfer.' There had been enquiries from the Belgian clubs Standard Liège and Anderlecht, and during the previous season West Bromwich Albion and Manchester United had also expressed an interest. A few weeks later, in an interview with the *Daily Mirror*, Cunningham even suggested playing 'on approval' for any interested party, citing the example of Barcelona player Hans Krankl who returned to play in his native Austria while still being paid by the Catalan club. 'They just can't fit him into their side,' he stated simply. Continuing in the same frank tone of the *El País* interview he says, 'As far as Real are concerned I've gone down the drain – but I'm close to total fitness now and I believe I've still got plenty to offer.' And poignantly he pleads for a fair hearing: 'I was never a rebel. People thought I had a chip on my shoulder because of my colour. But that's wrong. They thought I was always raving it up at discos. That was wrong.' The article also showed photographs of Cunningham wearing a sharply cut dark suit on the streets around the Bernabéu, leaning on a white sports car in one and elegantly smelling a rose in another. The lead picture, taken by photographer Monte Fresco, showed a near-naked Cunningham sitting on a treatment bench with his heavily scarred and disfigured knee to the fore, peering forlornly into the lens.

The publicity eventually paid off when a familiar name came calling in March 1983. His old manager at West Bromwich Albion, Ron Atkinson, now in charge at Manchester United, enquired about a loan deal to bring Cunningham to Old Trafford as a replacement for the winger Steve Coppell, who had been forced into early retirement. A deal was agreed until the end of the season, providing Atkinson with a cost-effective solution to his problem by signing a player he knew and liked and who also had something to prove. Atkinson knew that the old lightning-quick player of Albion days was gone for good and aware that he needed to be nursed slowly back in to first-team football. As he was put through his paces at the Cliff training ground, Cunningham was reunited with a couple of old teammates from Albion, Bryan Robson and Remi Moses, two of the brightest talents of a United side that was undergoing reconstruction under Atkinson. By April Cunningham was fit and ready to play again after almost a year out of action. He made his Old Trafford debut against Watford as a substitute and made a positive impact when a sweetly struck volley from a corner helped United to a 2–0 victory.

As the season entered its final stage he started against Norwich City and played a full ninety minutes without any adverse reaction. After four games in the first team he could at last allow himself to believe again: 'I've convinced myself that I still have a future in this sport', he remarked. In an interview with the Spanish press he said, 'If Manchester United want to retain me for next season I am ready to stay here, even though I know I will lose money in relation to what I would earn at Real Madrid. If it's right that my time in Spain is finished, I would be upset ... After all the problems adapting, then I started getting injuries as well. Things just started to go from bad to worse.' Adding rather incongruously, 'I would never say I haven't enjoyed myself at Real, and the club have not only treated me phenomenally, they've also helped me mature on and off the pitch. It's unjust, but if I do leave it will be United fans who will see the real Laurie Cunningham.' He was clearly in a delicate position and reliant on the goodwill of Madrid to release him from his contract and sell him on at an affordable price. Promising to show United fans 'the real Laurie Cunningham' may have sounded like bravado but it might also have been an attempt to convince himself that he was still up to the task of playing football at that level. Atkinson was more equivocal: 'He's still not the Laurie that I knew ... We'll have a look at him closely and see his evolution during the rest of the loan period and only then will we look at maybe bringing him to the club.' He played one more game before the end of the season and United finished third, twelve points behind champions Liverpool.

But the season was not over yet as United had reached the FA Cup Final against Brighton, just relegated from the First Division. Cunningham had put himself in contention for a place in the starting eleven, but, rather than enthusing him, the prospect of playing in the final at Wembley seemed to eat away at his self-belief. Confidence seemed to evaporate and when Atkinson gave Cunningham the nod after a late fitness test, he hesitated and complained that a hamstring injury sustained a few weeks earlier had not fully healed. He told his manager, 'I'm not 100 per cent ... don't play me, I could let you down.' In reality it wasn't his hamstring; psychologically he had given up before the match had even kicked off. Two years of injury and surgery had caused him to lose faith in his own ability. He later reflected: 'It seemed too good to be true for me to go from playing for Real Madrid, to a month later, being in a cup final for the next greatest team in the world. I felt I was taking someone's place.'

Manchester United decided not to pursue the loan deal any further and sign Cunningham permanently. Atkinson liked his teams to play quick, attacking football and, as he said, the old marauding Cunningham was now in the past. It was hard to justify the high fee Madrid would undoubtedly require for him as well; if he had been a free agent perhaps things might have been different.

Back in Spain again and surplus to requirements he must have felt redundant. He was still only twenty-seven and had a year left on his contract but was stuck in a catch-22 situation. He needed valuable match time to build up his confidence and showcase his talents to other clubs, but could not get selected by the manager. Taking matters into his own hands he contacted a number of Spanish clubs through his friend John Fitzgibbon who rang round on his behalf to gauge interest. Fitzgibbon got a good response from the Sporting Gijón president Manuel Vega-Arango and arranged a meeting for the player. Fortunately a familiar face was manager at the club – his old Madrid boss Vujadin Boškov – and quickly agreed to take Cunningham on a year's loan after some nimble paperwork registering him as a Castilla player was hastily arranged to smooth the progress of the deal.

Boškov had always liked Cunningham's inventiveness as a player and must have thought he still had something to offer. Though not a big club, Gijón had finished runners-up in the league in 1979 and been finalists in the Copa del Rey in 1982, and were a solid outfit. Situated on the north-west coast at the foot of the Bay of Biscay, the city was cloudy and wet more often than not and lacked the heat and glamour of the capital. They played their home matches at El Molinón, the oldest professional football ground in Spain. It would take some adjusting but Cunningham was at least back where he felt wanted by a manager whom he had previously praised for helping him to mature on the pitch. His delighted new president trumpeted him as a 'never before seen spectacle'. By the end of the season Gijón with Cunningham had finished thirteenth in a league of eighteen, hardly a resounding success, but at least he had proved to himself that he could last the pace. He played thirty out of thirty-four league fixtures, and scored three goals. The standard of football may have been a step down in quality but overall he must have been pleased just to be fit and playing again.

At the end of the season Cunningham's contract with Real Madrid finally expired and he moved on once more, this time to Olympique de Marseille in France on a free transfer. Again he played a full season (and scored eight goals) but by now his personal life had become complex. John Fitzgibbon started to receive phone calls at the *Sportsman* from a woman in Gijón asking for his whereabouts. It transpired that Cunningham had had a relationship with a woman called Maria Aurora Montes during his time there. She accompanied him to France and gave birth to a daughter on 3 July 1985 named Georgina Iona (Iona was his mother Mavis's middle name). He acknowledged paternity but disputed Maria's claim that they had married in London a year earlier. The long and the short of it is that he abandoned mother and child shortly after the birth and returned to Madrid, to Las Matas, where – in an eccentric living arrangement – he at one point shared the house with a troupe of dancers from a popular TV show. Fitzgibbon recalls the place as being a mess: 'He started knocking down walls but never completing it, it was a big open space with expensive furniture but he left it unfinished.'

Once home again, Cunningham promptly cut Montes and the baby out of his life, callously advising her that if she wanted to make some money she could always sell her story to *Marca*. Thereafter he steadfastly ignored her attempts to contact him. The article, a back-page exclusive, showed a photograph of Cunningham holding his newborn daughter above the headline 'Cunningham did not attend baptism of his daughter'. A bitter Montes told the reporter to 'tell everything, I'm tired of covering for Laurie to the press.'

Ever since he was a young man others had picked up on a certain remote, unreachable side to Cunningham's personality. He hated confrontation in his personal life. When he first went to Spain he was happy to leave business meetings and financial decisions to his girlfriend, as if his mind was elsewhere or he preferred not to be involved. As a teenager, his character quirks could be ascribed to innocence or unworldliness but as a grown man the disregard he showed to his 'wife' and child reflected badly on him.

In Madrid, a city he had grown to love, his remarkable career had dissolved into a protracted and frustrating ordeal. For most of it he was tied to a contract with a club that no longer wanted him and the cold facts of being a well-paid but expendable footballer at Real Madrid were hard to take. Of course it affected him; it even destroyed his confidence for a while. The career of a footballer is short and Cunningham was entering the final phase of his. After five fitful years at the biggest club in the world he was in danger of becoming just another ageing European journeyman.

8

NEVER GROW OLD

It's Friday night in Malasaña, a popular and colourful district in Madrid filled with young people looking for a good night out. A car playing loud dance music briefly parts pedestrians in the middle of the road as it nudges its way along the narrow street. As it slowly passes stragglers split and reform to continue their shuffling progress along the road. The restaurant I am looking for is situated beyond a lively crossroads with people spilling on to the narrow pavement from tiny tapas bars, or sitting in the window seats of the cafes on the corner. I have come to meet Sergio, who works in the restaurant, and his mother, Silvia, the son and widow of Laurie Cunningham. Having arrived early I order a beer and sit with a clear view of the door. I have only ever seen inky photocopies of press pictures of Silvia taken way back in the 1980s and a Facebook mugshot of Sergio which didn't tell me much about either. As the restaurant fills up I look at my watch and remember that the Spanish often don't eat until after 10 p.m. Presently I spot a couple coming through the front door being warmly greeted by the waiting staff.

I recognise Sergio first. Slim and handsome, he has his father's thick eyebrows, brown eyes and is sporting a goatee beard similar to the one his father occasionally wore. Casually dressed in a blue gingham shirt and jeans he offers me a cheerful handshake. After the deadpan photocopies

I had been used to looking at, Silvia is much prettier in person. Petite and chic in a pale linen blouse and trousers and swathed in an elegant necklace she has dark eyes and short, dark hair. We sit and Sergio orders platters of food and wine; as we get past the introductions it isn't long before he produces a book to show me. It is a copy of Cyrille Regis's autobiography with the author's inscription that reads: 'Your dad was an inspirational footballer, a barrier-breaker, a role model to thousands of young black footballers and a great and much loved friend to me.' Any fears I may have had about how forthcoming either would be are eased and it soon becomes obvious that they are happy to talk about Laurie with me.

I have brought with me a couple of British magazines that contain articles on Cunningham and I pass them across the table to Silvia. She looks at them with a quiet smile and a giggle then turns to the table behind her; it transpires it is occupied by a group of her girlfriends and they cackle with laughter at the photos in the magazine, especially the one of a young Cunningham in his Gatsby suit. Smiling, she returns the compliment and hands me some pictures of her own – among them Sergio as a toddler in his father's Real Madrid shirt and later on as a youth swamped by the voluminous Wimbledon kit his father wore in the 1988 FA Cup Final, and one of herself with Cunningham wearing a typical big 1980s leather jacket.

Silvia Lopez was born and grew up in Madrid and loved fashion as a girl. 'I was always crazy about clothes,' she admits and after leaving school worked in a clothes shop. That passion never left her and today she sells clothes from her own shop on Calle Serrano, one of the smartest streets in the city. She met Cunningham (she pronounces his Christian name 'Lowry') at a girlfriend's birthday party after he returned to the city in 1985 but had no idea that he was a celebrity. 'My friend said that he was a famous footballer but I didn't have a clue!' she laughs. So what attracted her to him? His looks? His clothes? 'No, his personality,' she replies, 'he was a very warm person, you felt comfortable as soon as you met him. He had a very special charm.' She uses the word '*entrañable*' to describe him, a brilliantly descriptive, incomparable Spanish word which literally translates as 'of the entrails' – when used fondly about a person it means you warm to them in such a visceral way that you feel it in your insides. I tell Sergio that he looks like his father and he says that a lot of people have told him that. 'When my English family see me they can't believe how like him I am. Same eyes. A bit taller.' Sergio also inherited his father's footballing skill and played for Real Madrid from the age of eight to thirteen and then for Atlético Madrid until he was sixteen. When I ask why he stopped he says he did not have enough self-discipline to fully commit to the game. He was quick and skilful but (he stands up to demonstrate the point) he couldn't take corners with the outside of his foot like his dad. I notice his hand is in plaster and he explains he injured a bone in it after smashing it on a table in frustration after Atlético had equalised against Real Madrid in the Champions League Final the previous Saturday night. Real Madrid won the match to give them eleven victories in the competition and after our meeting I see he has posted some footage online of himself and some friends, celebrating the team's trophy parade through the streets of Madrid in an open-top bus.

Although Silvia's family were not football fans they knew who Cunningham was. Her father, who had travelled widely in the navy, warned her that she might have problems with racism and advised her to think about how people would react to a mixed couple. He told her about the time when he was a young man in New York and a black woman laden with bags boarded a bus he was on. He offered his seat and was told by friends 'don't do that she is black', but he ignored them and gave up his seat. She says that the fact Cunningham was famous was of more interest to people than the colour of his skin whenever they went out; and laughs when I ask her if he liked Spanish music, 'No! Nor Spanish cinema!' but she adds he admired Spanish dance. 'He even danced Sevillianas (a form of Flamenco) which was very fashionable at the time. Laurie didn't know how to dance it properly but he would dance … we went to a *tablao* called El Porton' (a *tablao* is a club where Flamenco is performed).

With Silvia, Cunningham found some much needed stability in his life at a crucial time. After returning to Madrid his lifestyle had become ever more chaotic. Silvia says her calm influence at this stage of his career benefited him greatly. They married in June 1986. She strikes me as an unassuming, equitable person but is scathing about his ex-Real Madrid teammate Goyo Benito – his dubious friendship with her husband and the role he played in selling the Las Matas house to Cunningham. She says her husband was 'too trusting' and feels that 'Benito really took advantage of him. The house was like the house in that film *The Money Pit*. He poured a lot of money into it ... It was badly built and needed a lot of repairs. It was a very bad investment but he didn't want to sell it because it was a spectacular house. It was sold after he died. Even though he was owed two million pesetas according to a letter, I had to pay six million to Benito to be able to put it up for sale. A journalist who came to talk to me said Real Madrid owed Laurie money and said you should do something about it, you should have confronted Benito but you are too discreet and low-key. My sister and I went to see Benito and he called us bitches ... Even though Laurie knew that he [Benito] had not behaved well, that he had cheated him, he never criticised him, it wasn't his style, he never talked badly of him.'

Cunningham began to see Silvia every day and soon brought her over to London to meet his parents. She recalls his father, Elias, as a 'nice man' who did not speak much when they met and loved listening to reggae music. Mavis was more talkative; it was clear she ran the house: 'His mother had made their living room like a trophy cabinet since he was young, he'd won a lot of cups at school, he was incredible at playing football and his parents thought he was a phenomenon.' He took her shopping for clothes around London, which she loved, and introduced her to the nightlife of the capital: 'He took me to a private disco where they played reggae and I adored how they danced.' It can't have been easy for her as she didn't speak English and understood little about football but she says she was happy. 'They say love is blind ... I just wanted to be with him you know, nothing else.'

That autumn Cunningham moved to Leicester City where he stayed for seven months, for the most part living out of a suitcase in a provincial hotel with Silvia. He made fifteen appearances but again old ligament problems interrupted his playing time. In an interview with the *Birmingham Post* from the period he sounded like a man who knew his best days were behind him. He cited West Brom's 5–3 victory over Manchester United in 1978 as the greatest team performance he was ever involved in, and his best individual performance as the 1980 Real Madrid victory over Barcelona. After that match, he claimed, 'The Barcelona president came straight up to me and offered me whatever money I wanted.' In the interview he resorts to the by now familiar line 'the best is yet to come' – but doesn't sound totally convincing and he counters the perception that he is an expensive risk: 'I want to come back quietly just to settle down and get my game right … I don't want people to think I am demanding a lot of money. I'm not. Just a normal wage.'

A few months later he spoke to the *News of the World* and complained that football in England had become more hectic and less technical since he had been away. Commenting on the progress of black players, he said, 'The racial thing was at its worst between playing for Arsenal as a schoolboy and joining Orient. No one wanted to give black players a break. They were really tough times,' and highlighted a lack of progress that prevented black footballers from moving up in the game in the same way as their white counterparts. 'Have you noticed how we've all dropped out of favour with England? And there are no black managers in the game. I wonder why. I am not a Black Power merchant but you can't help feeling there is still prejudice. I don't think black players have had a fair deal over the years. They don't seem to be especially well paid.' He reflected on his own experience that, despite winning the Spanish League and Cup Double with Real Madrid and reaching the European Cup Final, 'it was out of sight, out of mind as far as Ron Greenwood was concerned.' It was unusual for Cunningham to speak out so directly and he made an important point about black managers – a problem that still exists today, more than thirty years later. The distrust of black players carried over into their post-playing careers. Most club chairman are still older white men and tend to rely on their networks when looking for managers; selection by interview was and still is rare, and appointments are often made after a personal recommendation. Cunningham's rhetorical question has never been properly addressed by football authorities. A survey by the Sports People's Think Tank (SPTT) at Loughborough University in 2015 found that in England just 4 per cent of elite coaching roles were held by black or ethnic minority people, despite 25 per cent of players coming from such a background, and calculated at the current rate of progress it would take thirty-one years before the figures accurately reflected the number of black or ethnic minority players in the professional game.

At Christmas 1985 Cunningham was interviewed by Central Television from his hotel in Leicester. The footage shows him and Silvia drinking tea from white china cups sitting beside an open fire. Much is made by the interviewer, in the introduction, of the exotic Englishman returning home after years in foreign countries, where presumably he had stopped drinking tea by the fireside. He tells the reporter that he would be interested in signing a contract if one was offered, and, speaking in Spanish in between questions, he continues that it's Silvia (who had given up her job to be with him) who is 'the most important thing in my life at the moment. I need her around ... I'm thirty, it's time for me to settle down.' His football career had become a peripatetic one, travelling around Europe but never staying anywhere for long. In such circumstances he needed someone to be with him permanently, who could bring a sense of order and direction to his frenetic life. Her calm, consistent personality was a palliative to the unpredictable world of football and supported him during a difficult phase in his career. 'He had to settle for less and it showed, he wasn't at the top any more, some days he was low,' she says of that time. He left Leicester in May 1986, and he and Silvia returned to Madrid to get married that summer as another season ended and once again he found himself without a club, not knowing what the new season would bring.

Rayo Vallecano were founded in Madrid in 1924. They play in the Vallecas area of the city – a proud eastern working-class suburb that has traditionally been an entry point for economic migrants to the capital from the south, including many gypsies from Andalucía. The area was a separate village for many years until it was incorporated into the greater Madrid conurbation in 1950. During the Franco years the neighbourhood earned its modern reputation for resistance and counter-cultural autonomy. It has kept its independent aura and the club's fervent supporters maintain a self-consciously radical, left-wing identity. Of the four main professional clubs in Madrid they are the most parochial and, with an ardent following, frequently punch above their weight. They are the polar opposite to the mighty Real

Madrid – in many ways they are the anti-Real – whose massive, towered Bernabéu stadium sits amidst the corporate glass skyscrapers of the financial district half an hour away on the metro. Rayo's *campo de fútbol*, a grime-streaked concrete box standing on a hill, is a more modest affair that incorporates the local swimming pool, boxing gym and a chess club. Its grey walls provide a canvas for some colourful hand-painted murals depicting the club's red lightning-flash logo declaiming '*valentia, coreja y nobleza*' – bravery, courage and nobility. Fly-posters announcing boxing bouts and stickers with communist symbols and anarchist imagery pepper the exterior walls. Cunningham, who had two stints at the club, between 1986 and 1989, is commemorated by a well-painted mural inside the ground showing him with the ball at his feet in the red and white Rayo kit beside the slogan '*Ama Al Rayo, Odia Racismo*' – 'Love Rayo, Hate Racism'. For the club's politicised hard-core supporters known as the *Bukaneros*, he is an inspirational maverick, a glamorous poster boy for tolerance and brilliance.

Cunningham must have recognised Vallecas, a multi-cultural, everyday neighbourhood, as similar to the part of London in which he had grown up. When I visit and emerge from the metro station beside the ground, I soon pass two young mothers in hijabs wheeling pushchairs on their way to a playground that bears a giant club logo painted on its far wall. I stand behind a group of schoolchildren waiting to cross the road, some – including a pair of girls – wearing the distinctive team shirt with its red lightning flash motif. I am instantly put in mind of the Seven Sisters Road at Finsbury Park where Cunningham grew up; it's a dowdy area of tower blocks, drying washing and small shops but with a distinct and interesting character of its own. Cunningham signed a year's contract with Rayo Vallecano and played thirty-seven games during his first spell there in 1986–87; anything more long-term was unlikely to be offered for a player of his age with such a chequered medical history. Rayo, a small club in a capital city with bigger, more glamorous neighbours – much the same as Leyton Orient in London – may not boast a roll call of honours but attracts a committed local following. Silvia remembers, 'He was in good form and it was clear the fans liked him. He really liked being back in Spain ... from the food to the people, the weather. Everything, he liked it a lot.'

Home life in Madrid suited Cunningham in this period but doubts about his career and the catastrophic investment in the house in Las Matas continued to nag. When Sergio was born in 1988, all three moved out to a rented apartment because of the impracticality of living in a house unfit for a newborn baby. 'It was really cold and expensive to heat and maintain, the pipes weren't done properly. Sergio was little so we only wanted one floor ... It worried him a lot. He saw that he hadn't made a good purchase, of course,' Silvia says. 'He was very trusting and made some bad deals,' to which Sergio interjects, 'I am just the same!'

Cunningham's season went well enough though he only scored three goals. His game had changed to a more tactical one in which he assisted rather than scored the goals and became creator rather than finisher. By 1987, however, he was a free agent once more and went on trial to the Belgian club Charleroi but it didn't work out and he played only one game for them. If a little-known Belgian club was an unexpected place to find the name Laurie Cunningham on the team sheet, his next move was even more surprising as he spent a short period at perhaps the unlikeliest club of all, Wimbledon FC, in London. Known as the 'Crazy Gang' for their outrageous off-field antics, they were a rough and tumble squad of players who became infamous for their no-frills, relentless style of football. A team that many purists despised for having dragged football back to the dark ages by terrorising the league with their physical hard-as-nails, in-your-face style of play. As England and Liverpool player John Barnes commented in later years, 'it was the most surreal thing ... it was the most un-Laurie Cunningham team to go to.'

I meet Bobby Gould in a coffee shop near Waterloo station, as he prepares for his weekly late-night football radio phone-in show. He is friendly and talkative. I want to speak to him about his time as Wimbledon manager and the most unlikely FA Cup victory – that defeat of Liverpool in the 1988 final. Luckily for me he is well-prepared and has brought his work diary from that year with him, a first-hand record of his thoughts and comments, the signings and deals of a remarkable year in the club's history. He opens the book and, tracing a finger across the columns, announces: 'Ah, here it is, he came to the club on Monday, 25 January 1988.' He received a call from an agent telling him Cunningham was looking for a club and went straight to the club owner Sam Hammam and told him: 'He'll be like a breath of fresh air. We had Dennis Wise, John Fashanu, Vincent Jones and Andy Thorne, we had our own culture and I just thought somebody with his technical ability, they could learn off him and he could learn off them.' Gould had lost winger Carlton Fairweather to a serious injury and needed cover for the rest of the season and says, 'I wanted someone with a bit of quality. I wanted him there to show them what natural ability was but, not only that, could he develop and play to a team pattern of play? We were second to none when it came to that.' He describes the system he and coach Don Howe developed that saw them flying high in the top half of the First Division by 1988. The system was based around getting the ball into opponents' territory at every opportunity in the most direct way possible, usually a long, high ball. The aim was for Wimbledon to get '172 "reaches" and 44 crosses per game, that is to "reach" the final third (the opponent's penalty area and its surrounds) 172 times in a game. That's what Dennis Wise and Carlton Fairweather had to do: get in 44 crosses in any game. [If you did that] chances were that you'd score and that's why people hated Wimbledon. They hated it! Especially opposition players, "Oh! here it comes again ... and again ... and again," there was no let up.'

The unique mentality among the players had grown during their ascent through the lower leagues and into the top flight under manager Dave Bassett, and Gould remembers his first team meeting in 1987 alongside Don Howe – a man who had coached both England and Arsenal. With the players gathered together for an introductory meeting Gould recalls, 'Me and Don got the flip chart ready, there's twenty-two of them and they have all been under Dave Bassett's culture and someone shouts out "No, no don't write anything" and four of them stand up – Dave Beasant, Alan Cork, Laurie Sanchez and Dennis Wise – and they came to the front and said "You are not coaching England now, you are coaching Wimbledon," and you have got to think of training sessions for playing that long ball into the other half, and that's how it started. They trained for hours on end and everybody knew their job ... midfield Sanchez and Jones, one touch and knock it back over, make them face their own goal. And they worked on free kicks and dead ball situations, the timing was perfection. We were all in it together and we were going to play long-ball football. That's what Cunningham came into.'

Flicking through his diary, Cunningham's name doesn't appear often and Gould suspects that may have been because of niggling injuries, which had cleared by March, when he is noted as being back in training with the first team. An entry for March indicates he signed him for a month on £500 a week. 'I was on £600, that's how much we wanted him,' Gould observes. I ask if he remembers what his behaviour was like with his teammates and he roars with laughter: 'Compared to that lot he was an angel! I think they couldn't believe that he'd come to the club. They were just in awe of him.' The team embarked on a successful cup run and after a semi-final victory at White Hart Lane against Luton Town reached the FA Cup Final for the first time in their history.

While preparing for the big game, the shrewd Howe told Gould he needed to change his wingers to stop Liverpool's key man, John Barnes, from playing. By having Wise and Cork switch sides, the tireless, energetic Wise could stick on Barnes so 'every time he looked up he saw Dennis' and the older, more experienced Cork could be freed to use his head more than his legs and be spared the task of having to track back to help in midfield. In the final training session before the game, Howe drilled the team with the change over of wingers and Gould continues, 'Cork and Wise practised penalties with goalkeeper Dave Beasant.' They had made a study of how Liverpool's centre forward John Aldridge took penalties. 'What happens Saturday afternoon? John Aldridge gets a penalty, who's the first goalkeeper to save a penalty in a Cup Final? Dave Beasant. It was their professionalism that won it. We had to make sure that we were going to influence the game, to nullify them.' That night, with tactics and game plan sorted, the squad went out for a meal in a restaurant, which Gould recalls descending into a noisy, unruly gathering: 'they started throwing bread rolls around the restaurant. I thought they won't last long in here so I got hold of Beasant and said, "Take them down the road there's a pub there, the Bunch of Grapes, here's £50 but nobody's allowed to have a pint in their hand." Cunningham was part of it and he couldn't believe it,' he laughs.

On the day Wimbledon scored early in the second half and spent the rest of the game holding on. With the clock ticking too slowly for comfort Gould had to make a decision and acted, 'I took Alan Cork off because his legs had gone, so that's where Laurie Cunningham came in. We were knackered, we were running dry. I didn't need anyone at the back because we were OK, but once we'd cleared the ball I wanted somebody to hold on to it and that's what he did for us. I told him, you do that and do your thing, do what you want in that top third but just track back. We had to make sure all the aces were covered you see.'

John Fashanu, a rangy, athletic centre forward, was the powerful target man of the side and played the game in a physical, aggressive way which earned him the nickname 'Fash the Bash'. He and Cunningham became good friends during his time at Wimbledon and his wife, Marisol, who was Spanish, hit it off with Silvia – the pair remain friends to this day although Marisol is no longer married to Fashanu. The post-match celebration dinner was held in a marquee erected on the pitch at Plough Lane, Wimbledon's home ground, where each player was allotted a table for guests and family. Gould can't remember much about Cunningham that night other than the fact that he was there: 'After that he left and went back to Spain,' he recalls. He had fulfilled the brief, and covered for Fairweather, and played his part in a memorable victory.

By September 1988 Cunningham was back at Rayo Vallecano in Madrid for his second spell at a club where he was held in high regard and was well treated. Looking at photographs from then, it is hard to recall the slight, lithe player of old. He is heavier set and looks fit but is physically more muscular and solid. He looks like someone who has spent as much time in the gym (doing rehab work) as he has on the football pitch. In a match early in the season he was put out of action after a challenge aggravated his damaged toe and the Rayo doctor advised him to consider a further operation. Two months later he was asked about the injury and quizzed on his memories of life at Real Madrid: 'They accused me of going to a nightclub to try and wash their hands of responsibility for my toe,' and, pressed on whether there was racism at the club, he answered, 'No I don't think so, but then as now, it's hard for a lad of colour to succeed in football … it's difficult to talk about this subject … a lot of specific journalists have done me a lot of damage with false stories.' In Spain, it seemed, he would always be defined as the playboy footballer who had sacrificed his gifts in favour of the dance floor. In a stop–start season, Cunningham made nineteen appearances as Rayo dramatically gained promotion to La Liga on the last day of the season. Across town a familiar face had turned up in the shape of Ron Atkinson, his former boss from West Bromwich Albion. Sacked by Manchester United in November 1986, and after another brief spell at WBA, he had been appointed manager at Atlético Madrid (and lasted just over ninety days before being dismissed by the temperamental club president Jesús Gil). One evening he went to watch Real Madrid at the Bernabéu with Cunningham and recalls the player leaning over to him and saying, 'Next year I'll show them what they've missed.'

By the summer of 1989, at the age of thirty-three, Cunningham was out of contract again but in negotiations to extend his stay at Rayo. If he could secure another year playing in La Liga it would be a satisfying and fitting way to finish his career, but problems off the field remained. Since leaving Real Madrid money had become an issue. A sense of grievance – that he had somehow been exploited by Real – surfaced in comments he made to friends and family. According to Silvia he also made some poor financial decisions and lost money in speculative ventures. He was unhappy about his treatment at Real and felt they still owed him money. The desperate situation with his house at Las Matas – he had shown potential buyers around it but to no avail – and the accompanying feelings of betrayal, continued to irk him.

One elusive acquaintance of Cunningham's was Mark Latty. Latty, a thirty-year-old American student living in Madrid, had been friends with Cunningham for some months and became his (rather spurious) business partner. Little is known about Latty, other than that he and Cunningham were involved in an enterprise together. Latty was the passenger in the car crash that killed Cunningham and was released from hospital a few hours afterwards. He seems to have left Spain soon after, presumably to return to America.

On the day before the crash, Friday 14 July 1989, Latty and Cunningham had spent the day together visiting restaurants with a view to buying one as a going concern. Later, as Friday turned into Saturday, they went to a private party at the O Madrid pizza restaurant. Perhaps it was on their list of possible acquisitions, but newspaper accounts reported that Cunningham was in a good mood as he drank sangria and chatted with guests. According to Latty, however, in the only interview with him I have been able to unearth about that night, he quickly became agitated after making a phone call and stormed out of the restaurant. 'He seemed annoyed about something but wouldn't say what.' Earlier that week Cunningham had made a further, slightly mysterious phone call to his mother, Mavis, asking her to lend him £200 to buy curtains for his house. Latty, who followed him out to his car and also got in, said he drove away at speed without putting his seat belt on in the direction of Las Matas on the La Coruña road at around 4.30 a.m. The La Coruña junction in the north-west of the city was a notorious accident black spot and no longer exists. As Cunningham approached the roundabout he accelerated around a slower car in front of him. As he did so he was instantly confronted by a car parked on the curve of the road where a driver had stopped to change a tyre. Swerving to avoid a collision he lost control, hit a lamp post and flipped the car over several times. He was thrown from it but Latty, who was wearing his seat belt, remained inside. He managed to free himself and crawl through a shattered window to call out to the parked car for help. Cunningham was found lying unconscious by the side of the road with a deep wound to his head, and rushed to hospital after a passing police patrol arrived at the scene. He was declared dead by doctors at 6.45 a.m. on Saturday 15 July 1989.

Cunningham's death was front-page news in the Spanish press and the eulogies from former teammates and club presidents were generous and numerous. Most remarked on his bad luck and his likeable, almost innocent nature. His former club president at Real Madrid, Luis de Carlos called him a star who had fallen to earth and his old teammate Juanito observed, 'He never had the luck he deserved, this accident sums it up.' The state news agency EFE remarked, 'The story of Laurie Cunningham is frankly sad and inexplicable', while the sports newspaper *El Mundo Deportivo* added that his career 'had been marked by bad luck virtually from the day he joined Real Madrid.' The newspaper *AS* declared that a 'black angel' had ascended to heaven. In England coverage was less emotive and harder to find and placed either in down-page articles or single column obituaries. He was a forgotten man after so long away and, although praised for his talent, his sudden death did not warrant in-depth coverage. A couple of titles quoted his old

West Bromwich Albion manager Ron Atkinson who called him 'arguably the best talent since George Best'.

Silvia recalls the whirlwind days after the crash. 'I had a terrible time. Soon after I found out on the news his mother found out and she called me up. She came straight over on a plane ... and then she asked me if he could be buried in London. I understood that because there is nothing worse than a mother burying her son. I accepted it, so we got to London and his mother wanted a second autopsy to be done. So the body was stored for fifteen days until his mother could have the second post-mortem and then he was buried. But I had to live it twice, here and there, with a fifteen day interval. So it was very long for me and very painful.' Mavis was convinced her son's death was suspicious. The phone call asking for money must have been alarming and she told a reporter, 'There is something wrong somewhere but I don't believe I will ever know the truth.' Silvia says that the post-mortem showed the impact of the steering wheel on Cunningham's chest was the fatal blow that killed him, even before he hit his head and that there was also a bite mark on his hand which Mavis was concerned about. 'She thought Latty had done it,' but she herself discounts any suggestion that her husband's death was anything more than an accident. 'It happened on a famously dangerous curve, he wasn't wearing a seat belt whereas Latty was.' She thinks that Mavis's reaction was due to shock: 'He was such a special son, she kind of lost her mind.'

The inquest into the death held at Hornsey coroner's court the following year found Cunningham to be three times over the drink-drive limit and recorded a verdict of accidental death.

The funeral was arranged for London and the service took place at Holy Trinity Church, Tottenham, on 2 August 1989. Speakers included Cunningham's grandmother, great-aunt, old friends, Cyrille Regis and Bobby Fisher, as well as Nikki, who recited some of his favourite poems. Ambrose Mendy gave the opening address and says today of his friend from all those years ago on Hackney Marshes, 'Without doubt he was the best black British footballer we've had. I can claim to know most of the high-achieving black players – Paul Ince, Ian Wright, Viv Anderson, Andy Cole, Garth Crooks, David Rocastle and John Barnes – he was the best of the lot because he had everything.' Silvia and Sergio stayed at Mendy's house while the second post-mortem was conducted and the coffin was changed to a silk-lined casket in keeping with Mavis's wishes. During this time sixteen-month-old Sergio became ill with bronchitis and was taken to St Mary's Hospital. Drained by the worry of Sergio's condition and the delay of a second post-mortem, Silvia recalls, 'I was distraught because I had to go through it twice. I had nightmares after seeing him embalmed in his coffin. It was an open casket, his face was intact. The mass made me cry a lot, they played gospel ... when we left in Ambrose's car he turned the radio on and it said we dedicate this song to Laurie. My sister and I burst into tears again. The gospel singing was so moving, Mendy was very kind and at the airport gave me some money for Sergio.'

As an outsider who did not know the family well, it is to Silvia's credit that she demurred to their wishes for the funeral service of her husband. Cunningham's family and oldest friends, including Nikki, were all present at the pulpit to give their tributes and eulogies. She got on well with Mavis and Elias and in their grief they became closer still. She was intimately involved in the funeral preparations and speaks movingly about the process of grieving and acceptance of death that she and the family endured. 'In the chapel of rest I dressed him and made him up in the casket because the undertaker made him look appalling, like a china doll, and I couldn't let his parents see him like that. In the West Indian tradition you have a wake for ten days and I sat beside the casket with a magazine and a glass of milk, which was ironic because we used to do that together. Meanwhile Mavis's house was full for three weeks … Mavis told me, "You have to go through the harshness of this, you have no choice." The night before he was moved to the church there was an all-night vigil.'

The vigil of prayer ended with the commencement of the service. 'Amazing Grace' and 'The Lord Is My Shepherd' were sung and finally, as 'Jerusalem' echoed around the walls, mourners were invited to file past Cunningham's casket. As the family prepared to line up, Nikki realised she was the last one left. 'I was left in this huge church all on my own and I said, "Where are you all going?" and Mavis said to me, "You have to close it [the casket]." So I was left alone, and it's funny the things you remember. I was given this doily by the priest to put over his face. It took me fifteen minutes to do it, to close it. And I walked outside and everyone was standing there. It was unreal.' The funeral party moved on to the cemetery and 'Abide With Me' was sung by the graveside as well as a chorus of gospel songs. Nikki recalls, 'We were at the graveside and everyone was singing. The gravediggers were given a rest and the men in the family had their jackets off and spades in their hands. There was non-stop singing. I got handed the first spade after the grave was dug. I didn't realise everyone was waiting for me to put the first piece of earth on the coffin. Cyrille handed me the spade and Elias on the other side said to me, "Make the first move, give us permission" ... I was waiting for them! ... Oh! Is that what we are waiting for? Mavis started singing "Where We'll Never Grow Old" whilst holding her grandchild and she sang for the whole time and everybody sang and it was wonderful.'

Three months after his death, on 1 October 1989, a memorial service was held for Cunningham at Southwark Cathedral. Among the 700 guests was England manager Bobby Robson. Rob Hughes, a long-standing champion of Cunningham since his days as a rookie at Leyton Orient, wrote in the *Sunday Times* about his significance to football on that day: 'Others now are getting their chance thanks largely to Cunningham's efforts and when Bobby Robson leaves Southwark tonight to work on his England squad ... he will be giving serious consideration to the inclusion of five black players: John Barnes, Des Walker, David Rocastle, Mickey Thomas and Paul Parker.' For Hughes, his impact was not limited to the football pitch either. 'Cunningham arguably became the sportsman who broke the prejudice affecting blacks on a British sporting field,' he declared and continued, 'In 1975, Don Revie, the then England manager, named eighty-four players under review for the national team. Not one was black. Neither were there any in the under-23 side or the youth and school teams, [and] I was told by twelve first division managers that they would not sign a black player because "they lacked bottle, were no good in the mud and had no stamina" – said at a time when Pelé and Eusébio had proved themselves the world's finest footballers.'

By the time of Cunningham's death the prospects for black professionals in Britain had improved. The emergence of a generation of exciting new talent was starting to make its way at the highest level of the game and spectacularly so in one instance. On 26 May 1989, fifty days before his death, a thrillingly dramatic match took place between Liverpool and Arsenal that decided the First Division championship. Arsenal, Cunningham's boyhood team who had rejected him as 'not the right material', beat Liverpool at Anfield – a ground where the young Cunningham had received such abuse that his manager had to take him off the pitch – in a memorable game. The match is regarded as a classic in English football. With only seconds left Arsenal were 1–0 up but needed to win by two clear goals to be crowned champions. As they launched one last desperate attack the decisive goal was famously scored by Michael Thomas – one of three black players on the pitch that night.

AFTERWORD

Laurie Cunningham's grave lies in a large cemetery in north London. The corner plot where he is buried is guarded by a huge, slouching pine tree, whose branches have shed most of their cones when I visit on a still October morning. The air carries a light chill as I sit down opposite his headstone to read the faded inscription before me: 'We loved you, but God loved you more', it says and at the foot of the grave the single word 'Laurie' is chiselled into the stone. The simple grave fits modestly alongside its more elaborate and decorative neighbours lined up in quiet rows.

Since I started writing *Different Class* in 2014 there has been a growing awareness about the importance of Laurie Cunningham. In the past year Waltham Forest Council have announced plans to erect a statue to him in 2017 at Coronation Gardens next to Brisbane Road, the home of Leyton Orient FC, the club where he first got his start.

In September 2016, on a sunny Wednesday morning, English Heritage unveiled a blue plaque in his honour outside the house where he grew up in Finsbury Park. He is one of only two footballers to receive such an honour; the other is the 1966 England World Cup-winning captain Bobby Moore. The plaque sits well on the front of the house on that unremarkable London street and states simply and elegantly: 'Laurie Cunningham 1956–1989 England International Footballer Lived Here'. When I first started researching Laurie Cunningham's story I was surprised that more had not been written about him in the numerous books about football in the 1970s. He seemed to be an unsung hero who had slipped through the cracks and become a forgotten figure – despite the fact he showed, with great flair and panache, that black players could be effective and succeed at the highest level. I mentioned this to Cyrille Regis when I met him and he wisely told me that one day he would be recognised for what he did. He said that often great artists are not recognised until after they have gone, that 'only time will tell'. I thought of that as I watched him on that sunny morning pull the cord to reveal the blue plaque above his old friend's childhood home.

ACKNOWLEDGEMENTS

I didn't set out to write a book about Laurie Cunningham when I first became interested in his story. My original intention was to put together an exhibition about him locally in the area of London where he grew up. For this book to take shape I have spoken with many people, all of whom I am indebted to for their insights, memories and help along the way and I'd like to thank the following.

The first person I interviewed was Cyrille Regis; approachable and friendly, he set the ball rolling and recommended others I should speak to and, if he hadn't been so honest and helpful, I probably would not have taken my interest any further. I was also lucky to meet Paul Gorman soon afterwards, a writer and cultural commentator; he immediately got why Cunningham was so important to me. Paul was full of interesting ideas and suggestions and viewed Cunningham through the prism of popular culture, which opened a door in my mind. It was his suggestion that I write a biography of Cunningham and he offered me generous help in putting together a book proposal – something I had never done before – and helped by providing diverse and relevant contacts for me to pursue. It was through meeting Paul and discussing my ideas with him that led directly to me writing this book.

I would like to thank the football writer Peter Law who was knowledgeable and helpful when we met. Peter, who sadly died in 2014, amassed an interesting archive of material on Laurie Cunningham and I am most grateful to his widow, Lesley, for letting me view it.

I'd also like to thank Sid Lowe, football writer and historian, who possesses a peerless knowledge of Spanish football and culture. He not only acted as translator for me when I visited Madrid but generously made his previous research on Cunningham available. He also attended the same north London comprehensive as Laurie by the way.

Of course I would like to thank the Cunningham family, especially Mavis Cunningham, for speaking to me so freely, a stranger who called her out of the blue one day from London at her home in Kingston, Jamaica. Thanks to Keith, June, Janet, Terisa and Rhodene for all their help too. And thanks to Laurie's Spanish family, his widow, Silvia, and son Sergio for their generosity and hospitality when I visited them in Madrid.

The moment I knew I was on to something special was when I discovered that Cunningham was so deeply involved in the London soul scene. The link was made with the help of Fitzroy Facey who was always helpful and responsive in answering my questions and gave me my first important contacts into that world. He edits a magazine called *Soul Survivors* which can be found at thesoulsurvivorsmagazine.co.uk.

I am grateful to Kick It Out and the Professional Footballers Association for supporting the book. Roisin Wood, the Director, and Lord Ouseley, the chair of trustees at Kick It Out, were encouraging as well as offering good practical advice. At the PFA Bobby Barnes, the Deputy Chief Executive, and Simone Pound, Head of Equalities, were equally supportive. Nikki Hare-Brown, Cunningham's girlfriend when he moved to Spain, was great to interview and the book would not have been half as good without her contribution. For his energy and enthusiasm I'd like to thank Mark Webster, original soul boy and general man about town (always on foot) who supported the book in various ways and notably got it in front of Adrian Rawden whose extremely generous backing came at the perfect time.

Many thanks to Ian Wright for writing the foreword. I had hoped that he was a fan of Laurie Cunningham but didn't know for sure – so it was great to find out that he meant so much to him when he was growing up in London; and thanks also to Lloyd Bradley, a writer whom I have long admired, for all his help as well.

I would also like to thank the following for their contributions: Toby Apperley, Dave Bowler, Nicola Baird, Steve Cottingham, Andrew Cowie, Gary Dennis, David Dodd of Leyton Orient Supporters Club, Bobby Fisher, John Fitzgibbon, Peter Gillman, Paul Gilroy, Bobby Gould, Leon Herbert, Rob Hughes, Eustus Isiae, Jah Wobble, Jazzie B, Colin Jones, Lloyd Johnson, Robert Johnson, Bert Jordine, Michael La Rose, Mark Leech, Don Letts, Gavin McOwan, Ambrose Mendy, Nicole-Rachelle Moore, Neville Murray, Dez Parkes, George Petchey, Mark Powell, George Power, Laurie Rampling, Ricardo the Mod, Evadne Ricketts, Steve Salvari, Matt Simpson, Martin Stern, Toby Walker, Dean Walton and Annabelle Whitestone.

Thank you to my agent Margaret Hanbury and her colleague Harriet Poland. And thanks to my publisher Unbound, who quickly got behind the idea of the book and just left me to get on with it. In particular I'd like to thank my editor Anna Simpson as well as Mathew Clayton, Phil Connor, Georgia Odd and Jimmy Leach for their help in guiding me through the whole publishing and crowdfunding process.

Dermot Kavanagh
October 2016

SUPPORTERS

Unbound is a new kind of publishing house. Our books are funded directly by readers. This was a very popular idea during the late eighteenth and early nineteenth centuries. Now we have revived it for the internet age. It allows authors to write the books they really want to write and readers to support the books they would most like to see published.

The names listed below are of readers who have pledged their support and made this book happen. If you'd like to join them, visit www.unbound.com.

Richard Ainsworth
Moray Allan
Robert Allen
Simon Amos-Melius
Ursus Arctos
Sam Ashurst
Sue Aston
Axminster Road Book Club
George Badchkam
Hilary Bagnall
Denzil Bailey
Jo Baily
Nick Baily
Patrick and Margaret Baily
Nicola Baird
Ashley Baker
Leighton Ballett

Paul Barber
Matt Barker
Gary Bass
Mark Baxter
Daniel Bayley
Mark, Lisa, Tom and
    George Beardmore
David Beauchamp
James Beech
Martin Belam
Michael Bell
Simon Bellis
Alan Berry
Warren Berry
Adrian Besley
Sanjay Bhandari
Robert Blenman

Edwin Blower

Ian Bolt

Mark Bourdillon

Toby Bourne

James Bowen

Sharon Bowen

Dave Bowler

Michael Boyd

Denise Brackell

Laurence Branigan

Everton A Brown

Nigel Bruce

Jane Bruton

David Bryan

Quentin Bryar

Finbar Bryson

Mike Buckland

Jerome Bull

John Burch

Andrea Butcher

Alistair Canlin

Sarah Carrick

Nick Cash

Ben Cawthra

Steve Cedar

Paul Chadney

Tom Chamberlain

Paul Charlton

Apala Chowdhury

Nick Clark

Jody Clayton

Suzy Clode

Richard Close

Marion Cole

Stuart Coles

Peter Collier

Rick Colls

Philip Connor

William Cook

Ian Corbishley

Nikki Cousins

Michael Cross

Noah Cullen

Rohan Daft

Anne Darlington

Stuart Davidson

Martin Davis

Jane Deacy

Chris Dean

Rajiv Desai

Nick Di Baggio Watson

Trevor Diner

Damian Donnelly

Lisa Donoghue

Mark Donoghue

Mohan Dosanjh

George Doughty

Graham Doughty

Remembering
    Calum Downes

Dermot Downey

Mel Doyle

Napoleon Dozier

Daragh Dunwoody

Jonathan Eden	Fred Guetin
Stephen Edwards	Patrick Gulliver
Roy Elliott	Nick Hadkiss
Jason Ellis	Matt Hall
Alan Emery	Steven Hallmark
Steve Emmins	Andy Hamilton
John Erratt	Margaret Hanbury
Neville Evans	Tim Haskey
Paul Fadoju	Kevin Hayes
John Ferguson	Adam Hearn
Mike Fitzgerald	Matthew Heggie
Paul Fitzpatrick	Keith Hemmings
Niall Flanagan	L.G. Henry
Paul Flower	Graham Higgins
Ugo Foraboschi	Alex Hill
Helen Foster	Bob Hill
Chris and Zeffy Foxton	Scott Hinchliffe
Dominic Franklin	John Hodgkiss
Ollie Fyfe	Paul Holt
Jason & Sharon Gale	Bernadette Horrocks
Paul Gallacher	Nick Horsley
Eddie Gershon	Andy Hunt
Peter Gillman	Paul Hunt
Paul Gilroy	Philip Ingles
Joseph D. Gongora	David Ivanov
Corinne Gorman	Jamie J
Paul Gorman	David Jenkins
Stephen Gough	Jess Jethwa
Robin Greedharry	Peter Johansson
Vanessa Green	Allison Jones
Jonathan Greenwood	Ben Jones
Ray Griffiths	Chris Jordan

Terry Jordan
Arthur Kavanagh
Hilary Kavanagh
John Kavanagh
Martin Kavanagh
Mick Kaye
Edward Kearney
Flea & John Keeble
Belinda Kessel
Graham
  Kettleborough
Dan Kieran
Ellena Kiki
Joe and Harry Klein
Stephen Lake
Ray Lakeman
Derek Lamb
Guy Lane
Andrew Lay
Jimmy Leach
Toby Leigh
Demelza Lightfoot
Nikki Lloyd
Brian Longman
Alan Love
Peter Lucas
Tanya Lyons
Luis Machado
Lachlan Macpherson
Cathie Mahoney
Brian Marple
Lee Marple

Dean Martin
Eileen Martin
Marina Martin
Alan Mayes
Andrew McDougall
Marc Mckee
Karin McKenzie
Sean Mckillop
Franklyn McNish
Claire Melamed
Steven Millington
Bob Mills
John Mitchinson
Bomber Morris
Graham Morris
Ian Moultrie
Nick Moyle
Sam Munday
James Murphy
Errol Murray
Carlo Navato
Steve Naventi
Julia Neall
Colin Newman
Eilidh Nic Sidheag
James Nichols
Michelle Nicholson
Carl Norman & Ella
  F Norman
John O'Donoghue
Eddie O'Kane
Sharon O'Neill

Dominic O'Reilly

Olusola Odemuyiwa

Raphael Olschner

Oliver Osmond

Sarah Overend

Gavin Paul

Muhammad Peart

Bob Penman

Chris Penny

Gerald Penny

Lucy Pepper

David Perkins

Erin & Grace Perry

Gordon Peterson

Justin Pollard

Frances Pope

Matthew Porter

Nigel Povey

Claire Powell

Gary Prail

Jeff Prestridge

Arron Probyn

David Proudlove

Brent Quigley

George Quraishi

Frank Radcliffe

Nick Randell

Gareth Rees

Cyrille Regis

Simon Rey

Neil Reynolds

Vaun Richards

Ian Ridley

Craig Robinson Old
   Incorrigibles F.C.

David Rouse

David Rutherford

Hesham Sabry

Gary Sanders

David Scally

Andrew Scott

Paul Seeney

Nicola Shears

John Sheehan

Simon Shipperlee

David Shrimpton

Lee Sidebottom

Matt Simpson

Ron Simpson

Neil Sims

Gary Sinyor

Andrew Sleight

Jackie Slotte

Louise Smith

Pierce Smith

Dave Sox

Angela St Hill

Sebastian Stanbury

Pete Statham

Kate Suiter

Lynda Sutton

Dr Andy Swallow

Liam Sweeney

Peter Tarry

Mark Taylor
Richard Thomas
Martin J Tickner
Kevin Tinmouth
Mark Townsend
Robert Truman
Paul Tuxworth
Phil Vasili
Liz Vater
Kosmo Vinyl
David Wallis
Liam Walsh
Paul Walters
Dean Walton
Charles Ware
Peter Warnell
Mark Waters
Robert Watson
Greg Watts
Guy Weaver
Paul Webster

Ray Wells
Nick Welz
John West
Graham White
Sarah Whitehead
Annabelle Whitestone
Peter Whyte
Donie Wiley
Jon Wilkins
Rich Wilkinson
David Willgoose
Luther Cornelius
    Mclachlan Williams
Paul Williamson
Ian Winrow
David Wright
Patrick Wright
Stephen Wright
Alan Wyle
Fawzi Zuberi